Be the Message

DEVOTIONAL

Books by Kerry and Chris Shook

One Month to Live

One Month to Love

Be the Message

Be the Message

DEVOTIONAL

A 30-Day Adventure in

Changing the World Around You

Kerry & Chris
SHOOK

WaterBrook
PRESS

BE THE MESSAGE DEVOTIONAL
PUBLISHED BY WATERBROOK PRESS
12265 Oracle Boulevard, Suite 200
Colorado Springs, Colorado 80921

Hardcover ISBN 978-1-60142-615-4
eBook ISBN 978-1-60142-616-1

Published in the United States by WaterBrook Multnomah, an imprint of the Crown Publishing Group, a division of Random House LLC, New York, a Penguin Random House Company.

WATERBROOK and its deer colophon are registered trademarks of Random House LLC.

Library of Congress Cataloging-in-Publication Data
Shook, Kerry.
   Be the message devotional : a thirty-day adventure in changing the world around you / Kerry and Chris Shook. — First Edition.
      pages cm
   ISBN 978-1-60142-615-4 — ISBN 978-1-60142-616-1 (electronic) 1. Witness bearing (Christianity) 2. Christian life. 3. Devotional literature. I. Title.
   BV4520.S4552 2015
   242'.2—dc23

                                                    2014038132

Printed in the United States of America
2015—First Edition

10 9 8 7 6 5 4 3 2 1

SPECIAL SALES
Most WaterBrook Multnomah books are available at special quantity discounts when purchased in bulk by corporations, organizations, and special-interest groups. Custom imprinting or excerpting can also be done to fit special needs. For information, please e-mail SpecialMarkets@ WaterBrookMultnomah.com or call 1-800-603-7051.

Contents

Open Yourself
to a dynamic encounter with God

Are you ready to receive God's message? Take a moment to settle down. Breathe. Try to put today's distractions out of your mind. In your own words ask God to meet you in this devotional time.

Open God's Word
to hear God's message

You study the Scriptures diligently because you think that in them you have eternal life. These are the very Scriptures that testify about me.

—JOHN 5:39

Open Your Mind
to understand God's message then and now

On nearly every page of the Gospels, Jesus has some sort of run-in with the religious leaders of His culture. This is astonishing when you think about it. These scribes and Pharisees committed themselves to the careful study of God's Word. They meticulously followed the rules they found there, and they urged others to do the same. But somehow they missed the point.

In this passage from John 5, Jesus gets to the crux of the matter. While the leaders were indeed experts in scriptural content—they would ace any Bible quiz—they were ignorant about the essence of God's message. It was ultimately about Jesus.

Were the "experts" right about finding eternal life in the Scriptures? Well, sort of. We do find life in the Scriptures, but not because we earn points for completing our reading assignments. We find life in God's message because we meet Jesus there.

Bible knowledge itself can't earn a spot in heaven, in the first century or the twenty-first. Sure, it's great to memorize verses and gather theological ideas, but the key is to encounter Jesus as we read and ponder.

Open Your Heart
to the divine whisper

Sit in silence for a few minutes. Imagine Jesus sitting with you. Enjoy His presence. Thank Him for meeting you in this quiet time.

Use this space to write down a simple prayer of welcome, thanks, and love.

_____

_____

_____

_____

_____

Open Your Life
to God's transforming power

Continue this conversation with Jesus by listening to what He has to say. Ask Him how you could please Him more. What changes does He want to make in your life?

Ask Him about today's Scripture passage. How would He apply it to your life? We often write off the scribes and Pharisees as judgmental hypocrites, and they were, but here Jesus says their problem was that they missed the point. They missed Jesus.

In our quest for biblical expertise, we can easily make the same mistake. In fact, sometimes our Bible knowledge can shield us from a genuine encounter with the living Christ. We explain things and categorize them instead of receiving a true challenge from the Lord. Ask Jesus what He thinks about that. What does He suggest you do to transform your Bible study?

Use this space to jot down what He seems to be telling you.

_____

_____

_____

_____

_____

Open Your Arms
to a world that needs to receive God's incarnate message through you

In His earthly ministry Jesus was always raising people's vision. "Lift up your eyes!" He *saw* the lepers and beggars who were routinely ignored by others, and He urged His followers to see them too. In His closing comments, just before He ascended, He even challenged the geographical myopia of His disciples, sending them outward to Samaria and "the ends of the earth" (Acts 1:8). Your life-changing interaction with Jesus may start in a small, quiet room, but it moves out to a world that desperately needs to connect with Him.

Today in your conversation with Jesus, name a half-dozen friends or associates whom you care about. Be sure to include some who, as far as you know, don't know Jesus yet. Include some who need help or healing.

Write down their names and any additional notes about their needs.

_____

_____

_____

_____

_____

Bring these names to Jesus. Ask for His truth to challenge them, His love to embrace them, and His healing touch to restore them. Don't be surprised if He asks for your help in some of this. Sometimes He invites us to participate in the answers to our own prayers.

Open Yourself
to a dynamic encounter with God

> May the words of my mouth
>> and the meditation of my heart
> be pleasing to you,
>> O LORD, my rock and my redeemer.
>> —Psalm 19:14, NLT

Open God's Word
to hear God's message

And when you pray, do not be like the hypocrites, for they love to pray standing in the synagogues and on the street corners to be seen by others. Truly I tell you, they have received their reward in full.

—MATTHEW 6:5

Open Your Mind
to understand God's message then and now

Apparently, in Jesus's day, prayer had become a spectator sport. He criticized the "hypocrites" who tried to impress others with their public show of devotion. The word *hypocrite* was actually used for actors, who in that time wore masks. Some masks had megaphones built in so the actors' words would not be muffled. And often the same actor would play several roles, using a different mask for each. Clearly Jesus saw through the acts of these pious posers.

For many people today religious devotion is still a show. They're trying to impress others with their piety rather than authentically bowing before the Lord. Note that Jesus didn't waste words in putting down such playacting. He simply said it was what it was. It was a show, a sham—a work of art, even—but it wasn't true prayer. Those hypocrites got the applause they sought and nothing more.

True prayer is an honest encounter with the living God. You're not performing—for Him or anyone else. You're just talking . . . and listening.

Open Your Heart
to the divine whisper

Sit in silence for several minutes, focusing on God, not on yourself. Yes, it's hard to be quiet, but this is not about how good you are at meditation. You are not trying to succeed at devotions. You are just opening your heart to God. If it helps, you might let certain phrases or images of God fill your thoughts. *God, You are loving . . . holy . . . faithful . . . a Rock . . . the Creator . . . a fountain of life . . . a feast of delight.*

Use this space to record some of these phrases.

_____

_____

_____

_____

_____

_____

_____

Open Your Life
to God's transforming power

Ask God to shine His spotlight on your life, not as a performer, but as a lab specimen. God is continuing His good work in you, growing you, transforming you, helping you conform to the image of Jesus. So let Him point out the falsehoods. Do you pretend to be more godly than you are? Are you satisfied with a public image of religious devotion rather than actually being devoted to the Lord of life?

A word of caution: Sometimes we Christians pride ourselves on being humble. We try to outdo each other by finding nitpicky aspects of life to improve. That can be just as much of an act as public oratory.

Bare yourself before God. Put down your mask. Let God see the real you, and let Him change you in the way He wants.

Listen for His guidance. Respond to His nudging. In the space below jot down what you hear Him saying about getting real with Him. And keep in mind that He might be saying, "Relax. Just *be* with Me for a while."

_____

_____

_____

_____

_____

Open Your Arms
to a world that needs to receive God's incarnate message through you

The Bible tells us that our good lives can be a beacon to others. But of course we are still sinners, and our lives are not always good. As a result, some of us make a terrible choice: we *pretend*. We assume we can still be a good testimony to others if we cover up our faults and pretend to be more righteous than we are. That is dangerously bad thinking.

We live in a world of strugglers. People grapple with guilt, doubt, disappointment, fear, and frustration. You live and work with people like this. They don't need to see a carefully manicured *portrayal* of a Christian life. They need to see a fellow struggler who authentically interacts with a very real God.

Take this time to talk with God about those people in your life. Is there anyone you need to be more honest with? How can you share the realities of your up-and-down life with such a person and be truly helpful?

Write down the names God brings to mind and what you can say or do.

_____

_____

_____

_____

_____

_____

Day 3

Open Yourself
to a dynamic encounter with God

Come away from the noise of life. Turn off the phone, the computer, the music . . . even if it's Christian music. Get quiet and listen for God's whisper.

Open God's Word
to hear God's message

The LORD said, "Go out and stand on the mountain in the presence of the LORD, for the LORD is about to pass by."

Then a great and powerful wind tore the mountains apart and shattered the rocks before the LORD, but the LORD was not in the wind. After the wind there was an earthquake, but the LORD was not in the earthquake. After the earthquake came a fire, but the LORD was not in the fire. And after the fire came a gentle whisper.

—1 KINGS 19:11–12

Open Your Mind
to understand God's message then and now

Elijah showed all the signs of a deep depression. He had just won the greatest victory of his life—literally a mountaintop experience—calling down fire from heaven to embarrass the false prophets. But that just made the evil queen more determined to kill him, and he ran for his life. To the desert. Where he sat. And slept. And sat.

God met him in his moping.

Hungry, tired, and disappointed that his great win hadn't really changed anything, he begged God to take his life. The Lord responded with the best object lesson ever, using "objects" like wind, earthquake, and fire.

These were great shows of force, but the Bible text says the Lord was not in any of them. Then came the "gentle whisper" of God—what older translations call His "still small voice."

The lesson for modern-day Elijahs is clear. Who cares about earth, wind, and fire when we can tune in to God's voice? When we are dizzy with the ups and downs of life, we will find God not in dazzling spectacle but in the quietness of a personal relationship with Him.

Open Your Heart
to the divine whisper

If you are disappointed or troubled or just weary, God will meet you there. He sits with you in the silence. He whispers His love. Quiet your soul and hear His gentle breathing. The New Testament describes this sweet interaction like this: "The Spirit himself testifies with our spirit that we are God's children" (Romans 8:16). Receive that reassurance.

Use this space to record what you sense the Spirit saying.

_____

_____

_____

_____

_____

_____

_____

Open Your Life
to God's transforming power

Do you seek dazzling displays of divine power when God just wants to hang out with you? Are you looking for a spiritual breakthrough, some deep insight or uplifting experience that will fuel your Christian life in the coming weeks and months?

It's not uncommon to want that. And, yes, God does some amazing things. He did send fire to consume Elijah's sacrifice on Mount Carmel, and He may have worked some miracles in your life too. But we humans have a tendency to worship the miracle rather than the God who made it happen. And when you think about it, is it really any more of a miracle to walk on water than it is for Jesus to walk beside you as you go through each day?

Ask God to help you tune in to His frequency. He can train you to hear His still, small voice as easily as you hear thunder. What do you hear him whispering to you now?

_____

_____

_____

_____

_____

_____

_____

Open Your Arms
to a world that needs to receive God's incarnate message through you

Are there people in your life who assume God has turned His back on them? Does their pain or depression put them in the place of Elijah—worn out, giving up, wondering what went wrong? Maybe they're daring God to prove His love with some great miracle.

Truth be told, sometimes God does exactly that. But often He chooses a quieter method. He uses people like us to be the miracle, to step into their lives with a message of love and hope.

Use this space to write down the names of such people and what sort of message they need to get from you . . . and from God.

_____

_____

_____

_____

_____

_____

_____

Open Yourself
to a dynamic encounter with God

Try this prayer as an entry into your quiet time.

> *You are a great God who loves and guides me.*
> *You are a great God who loves me.*
> *You are a great God.*
> *You are God.*
> *You are.*
> *You.*

And then rest in the silence, letting Him fill your heart with all that He is.

Open God's Word
to hear God's message

> He says, "Be still, and know that I am God;
>   I will be exalted among the nations,
>   I will be exalted in the earth."
>   —Psalm 46:10

Open Your Mind
to understand God's message then and now

Psalm 46 is quite noisy actually. War and natural disasters threaten the faithful. Nations are in an uproar. Mountains are sliding into the sea. Despite the tumult, we don't need to fear, because God is our refuge. He helps us.

So the stillness is not the product of a boring existence. On the contrary, stillness is a choice we make in the middle of this disaster movie we call life. We choose not to add our anxious screams to the noise around us. We will trust God no matter what else is going on. We will take the risk of resting in Him.

Stillness is not an end in itself. Sitting quietly and taking deep breaths might lower our blood pressure, but that's not the point here. The point is to know that our Lord is God, that He has ultimate control over the chaos around us. The Creator of all has charge over what He has made. Amazingly enough, He still wants some quiet time with us.

Open Your Heart
to the divine whisper

Pray today's verse back to the Lord. *I am still, Lord. I want to know You. You are my God. I will exalt You in my world.*

Leave some time between the phrases, and let the Lord fill in the blanks. What does He want you to know about Him? What does it mean for Him to be your God, especially in the tumult of your life?

Jot down any thoughts He brings to mind.

_____

_____

_____

_____

_____

_____

Open Your Life
to God's transforming power

How good are you at *being still*? Some of us need to be on the go all the time. Maybe even this devotional time is being crammed into a corner of the schedule between one meeting and another. There are just too many things to do! Others have a lighter schedule.

But mere stillness isn't the goal—it's what we do with it. God invites us to take this time to get to know Him better. What does that mean in your life, whether you are racing from one event to another or sitting at home playing computer games? Can you set aside quality time with God? Will your deepening knowledge of God bring order to your crazy life? Or will it bring purpose to a boring life?

Right now listen to God's ideas about how you spend this time with Him—and how that might affect the rest of your life.

_____

_____

_____

_____

_____

_____

_____

Open Your Arms
to a world that needs to receive God's incarnate message through you

Be on the lookout for frantic people, those who chase through life fretting about what will happen if they don't keep up. How can you bring the truth of today's verse into their lives? Can you encourage them to slow down, to be still, to take a break and breathe for a minute? How can you do this?

And don't stop there. In the stillness they can gain a sense of God's ultimate control over the chaotic events of their lives. Some of these frantic people will be Christians. Maybe you can remind them of what they already know—that their beloved Lord is still in charge. But God will also bring unbelievers across your path, people who fill their lives with activity because they see little else to live for. What can you do to show them that their Creator cares for them?

Jot down the names of those God might want you to slow down for a moment. What word of comfort might you have for them?

_____

_____

_____

_____

_____

_____

_____

Open Yourself
to a dynamic encounter with God

"Same old same old." That phrase was common a few years ago, often in answer to the greeting "What's up with you?" "Same old same old." How depressing is that!

Sadly, our devotional times with the Lord can sometimes decay into a same-old-same-old monotony—read a verse, then say a prayer, Amen. Get 'er done and get on with your life.

Let's put an end to that today. Are you ready for God to do something new in your life, starting now? Are you?

Open God's Word
to hear God's message

Forget the former things;
    do not dwell on the past.
See, I am doing a new thing!
    Now it springs up; do you not perceive it?
I am making a way in the wilderness
    and streams in the wasteland.
      —Isaiah 43:18–19

Open Your Mind
to understand God's message then and now

This section of the sprawling book of Isaiah was clearly written for suffering people. The people of Judah were carried off into captivity and languished for several decades in Babylon—far away from their homeland, from their traditions, from their temple. Miles of desert separated them from anything familiar. Spirits were crushed, identity shattered, faith challenged. As a psalmist put it, "How shall we sing the LORD's song in a foreign land?" (Psalm 137:4, NKJV).

This was a crucial time of self-examination and repentance for people who had drifted far too easily into idol worship, greed, and corruption. But now the Lord was drawing a sharp dividing line between past and future. *That was then; this is now. I am doing a new thing, creating a path through the desert.*

Historically, this actually happened. A stunning shift of power and policy gave God's people a chance to return to Israel. They had the opportunity to set up a new nation on their old territory. As another psalmist described the reaction, "Our mouths were filled with laughter, our tongues with songs of joy" (Psalm 126:2).

God still does new things for His people today. He paves pathways through the deserts of our lives. Perhaps you've been dwelling on past mistakes. Now God tells you, "Forget about it! Let Me do something new with you."

Open Your Heart
to the divine whisper

Thank God for forgiving your sin. Take some time to bask in His great love.

There's some blank space below, but *don't* write in it. That's where you would write down the sins of your past—if they still mattered. God has forgiven them. What's past is past. Review His assurance that He has removed your sin "as far as the east is from the west" (Psalm 103:12).

_____

_____

FORGIVEN

_____

_____

Now ask Him for the courage to move forward, letting go of past regrets and following Him into a new adventure . . . starting at this moment.

Open Your Life
to God's transforming power

Newness can be scary. We sometimes find comfort in clinging to our old ways. Even our old regrets can feel familiar. We know how to be sorry for past errors. We might not know what sort of courage we will need for the future.

What kind of attitude adjustment is necessary to welcome the new life God wants for you? Forgetting the past requires mental and spiritual discipline. It takes faith to step forward into God's new direction. How will God nurture that spirit in you—and help you let go of what haunts you?

Write down anything He's telling you about this new attitude He's awakening in you.

_____

_____

_____

_____

Open Your Arms
to a world that needs to receive God's incarnate message through you

Think of the people you see every day who are weighed down by past regrets. Sometimes you see this in their physical appearance—they seem to carry the weight on their shoulders—but sometimes you just sense it in their souls. How can you ease that burden? How can you be an agent of God's newness?

You might start among those with whom you have a history. Are there people you need to forgive? Do you need to make it clear to them that they are forgiven?

Are there others who just need the reassurance of God's forgiveness for mistakes they have made? Bring today's verse with you as you offer them peace for the past and excitement over the new thing God can do in their lives. What people do you need to contact, and what will you say?

_____

_____

_____

_____

Open Yourself
to a dynamic encounter with God

"I have loved you with an everlasting love," the Lord tells us (Jeremiah 31:3). As you enter this quiet time with Him, step into that love.

Open God's Word
to hear God's message

Call to me and I will answer you and tell you great and unsearchable things you do not know.

—JEREMIAH 33:3

Open Your Mind
to understand God's message then and now

When he received this message from the Lord, the prophet Jeremiah was under arrest for warning God's people of impending judgment. The authorities didn't like his negativity. He was seen as a traitor, a domestic terrorist.

Jeremiah was in a tough spot—hated by his own people for telling the truth. He often complained to God about this, but God kept him on the job. The promise in today's verse serves double duty. On one hand, it's reassurance for the frustrated prophet. *You might not understand what's going on right now, but keep in touch with Me, and you'll learn more and more.*

On the other hand, it could be an invitation to the people at large. Throughout Scripture, God implores us to communicate with Him, even if it's just a cry for help. When we open this interaction with our Creator, He blows our minds with "unsearchable" knowledge. The Hebrew word for "unsearchable" is sometimes used for walled cities—inaccessible to passersby but open to the one who is welcomed in.

God wants to welcome us into His mysteries. It doesn't mean we have secret knowledge that makes us better than others. It's more like a perspective in which the Spirit applies God's wisdom to the events of our lives. That starts when we call to Him in the midst of the challenges we're facing.

Open Your Heart
to the divine whisper

Sit in silence for a minute or three. Imagine the treasures of God's wisdom as a walled city with the gate opening to welcome you. In your own words, in your own way, call to Him.

In this space you may want to write down (or draw?) some thoughts or images.

_____

_____

_____

_____

_____

_____

_____

Open Your Life
to God's transforming power

How often have you found yourself in "impossible" situations—trying to do the right thing but hampered on all sides? People misunderstand your good intentions. You might even doubt yourself. What does God want from you? Why did He put you in this no-win situation? Couldn't He find anybody, you know, *qualified*?

Welcome to Jeremiah's world.

No, you don't have the answers, but God does. We all like to push through the challenges and emerge victorious on our own steam, but that's not the key to success here. We need to call on the Lord for help. We need to turn things over to Him and then let His wisdom change us and transform our situation.

How do you see this change happening in your life? Do you find it hard to call on God for help? What will that prayer sound like?

_____

_____

_____

_____

_____

Open Your Arms
to a world that needs to receive God's incarnate message through you

Our world is full of Jeremiahs laboring for God in tough circumstances and prone to discouragement. Take a few moments to think about and pray about the people you know in church ministry—whether pastors or lay workers. Then think and pray about any missionaries you know, in foreign countries or closer to home. Is God bringing any of these people into your heart right now, anyone who might need a special word of encouragement from you?

You know, after God invited Jeremiah (and the people) to call on Him, He issued a warning about hard times to come. But then there's a promise: "I will heal my people and will let them enjoy abundant peace and security. . . . I will cleanse them from all the sin they have committed" (Jeremiah 33:6, 8).

Jot down the names of any modern Jeremiahs that God is asking you to encourage. What will you say to them?

_____

_____

_____

_____

_____

_____

_____

Open Yourself
to a dynamic encounter with God

As you come to this time with the Lord, present yourself to Him fully—body, mind, and spirit.

Open God's Word
to hear God's message

In the beginning was the Word, and the Word was with God, and the Word was God. He was with God in the beginning. Through him all things were made; without him nothing was made that has been made. . . . The Word became flesh and made his dwelling among us.

—John 1:1–3, 14

Open Your Mind
to understand God's message then and now

In the Bible's first chapter, God speaks things into being. He calls for light, and there's light. By His word the sea and sky divide. This is, no doubt, the creative power that John was referring to in his opening chapter. The spoken word was indeed "with God" in the creation of the world, but when John talked about "the Word," he meant more than a collection of sounds or syllables. The Greek word *logos* can mean a spoken word, but it can also be translated "idea" or "reason." It was a favorite of some Greek philosophers, who saw the whole universe operating according to some superspiritual principle. They would have loved what John was saying here . . . until he got to verse 14.

They would have found it shocking that the overarching *logos* that ran the universe would take on flesh and blood, but that's exactly the point. John went on to introduce Jesus, the poor rabbi who was also the sacrificial Lamb of God and the cosmic energy behind all creation.

Sometimes Christianity is treated as merely a philosophy, an idea, a set of guidelines for behavior, a theory of existence. And maybe it can be all those things, but at its core is this stunning miracle: the *logos* became flesh. It is the divine power of the Creator becoming human, entering His creation, and living among us.

Open Your Heart
to the divine whisper

Here's a thought: instead of merely mulling over these ideas mentally, why not get your body involved? The Word became physical, so perhaps that calls for a physical response. Take a walk, do a dance, raise your hands, or kneel. Let your body honor the incarnate Lord.

After you do this, you might want to write down a few things about it. Did you connect with the Logos in a new way?

_____

_____

_____

_____

_____

_____

Open Your Life
to God's transforming power

Our culture worships physicality. Appearance is everything. Beautiful people dominate the media, and if you are not whipping your body into shape, well, what's wrong with you?

In answer, some Christians ignore the physical, focusing only on feelings, thoughts, and spiritual experiences. But Scripture keeps guiding us into an *incarnational* faith. As Jesus was the Word made flesh, we, too, can put our words into action. Praying for people is good, but we're also told to care for their tangible needs (see James 2:14–17). We don't just hear God's Word; we put it into practice (see James 1:22).

We need to develop an incarnational instinct—or rather to let God develop it in us. This does two things: it resists body worship by valuing people at a soul level, and it promotes the physical expression of our spiritual commitment.

How will God develop this incarnational instinct in you?

_____

_____

_____

_____

_____

_____

_____

_____

_____

Open Your Arms
to a world that needs to receive God's incarnate message through you

When the Word became flesh—Jesus—He helped people physically as well as spiritually. He challenged His disciples, then as well as now, to join Him in this ministry. We know that people need to know Him, but they also need food, clothing, shelter, and often healing.

Ask God to open your eyes to some physical need in the world around you. What can you do to help? Sometimes the easiest way to meet the need God brings to your attention is to send money to a worthy organization, but we encourage you to consider a different approach as well. In what ways can you use your flesh and blood to help someone in need?

_____

_____

_____

_____

_____

_____

_____

Open Yourself
to a dynamic encounter with God

"Open the eyes of my heart, Lord."

Come to Him today, ready to see things in a new light.

Open God's Word
to hear God's message

Before long, the world will not see me anymore, but you will see me. Because I live, you also will live.

—JOHN 14:19

Open Your Mind
to understand God's message then and now

Everything would be changing soon for Jesus's disciples. In His farewell talk, shared at the Last Supper, the Master prepared His followers for the tumultuous events ahead. He would be going away. He spoke about His crucifixion and burial in the near future, but He was also looking ahead to His resurrection and ascension. He would no longer be walking the paths of Judea or Galilee with them, but He would send them a Counselor, who would continue His work in them. Jesus would no longer be physically present with them, but He would be present through His Spirit.

Today's verse offers some rich insight into this situation. After Jesus ascended to heaven, the world, with its physical perspective, would no longer see Him, but His disciples would. They would see Him through the Spirit, who would live in them. Of course this is talking about us too. Jesus is as real to us as if He were standing beside us, because the Spirit opens our eyes to a new reality.

But wait, there's more. Because Jesus is still alive, we also have life. The eternal life He promised has already started for us. We can live in an eternal kind of way, with an eternal perspective and eternal priorities. In fact, the Bible indicates that Jesus is now living His life through us. We are His hands and feet. The incarnate Lord is *still* incarnate—living in *our* bodies.

Open Your Heart
to the divine whisper

Let that concept seep through your mind and spirit. Wave your hand. Tap your foot. That's Jesus's body waving and tapping. Jesus lives in you. How does that make you feel?

_____

_____

_____

_____

_____

Open Your Life
to God's transforming power

This idea—the Spirit of Jesus alive within us—gives rise to the later biblical idea of us as the body of Christ. That's more than a metaphor.

The Christian church is the physical force through whom Jesus operates. But another passage develops this further. Collectively and individually we are the temple of the Holy Spirit. Since the Spirit of Christ lives within us, our behavior should be in keeping with the Spirit's desires.

We often view this from a negative angle: "Be careful, little hands, what you do." But we can also rejoice in the positive aspects of housing the Spirit. We have energy, we act with meaning, and we serve a higher purpose, all because our lives are connected intimately with the life of Christ.

How will this affect how you think and what you do?

_____

_____

_____

_____

_____

_____

Open Your Arms
to a world that needs to receive God's incarnate message through you

If Christ is now living in you and through you, how will that affect your actions *toward others*? With the blood of Christ pumping through your veins, will you work to bring people to redemption? Since your sinews now belong to the Healer, how will you reach out to help others? Are there friends to visit in the hospital, meals to make for a struggling friend, or ways to promote justice for poor people around the world?

Your eyes belong to Jesus now. What needs is He showing you?

_____

_____

_____

_____

_____

_____

_____

Open Yourself
to a dynamic encounter with God

> Praise the LORD, my soul;
>> all my inmost being, praise his holy name.
> Praise the LORD, my soul,
>> and forget not all his benefits—
> who forgives all your sins
>> and heals all your diseases,
> who redeems your life from the pit
>> and crowns you with love and compassion,
> who satisfies your desires with good things
>> so that your youth is renewed like the eagle's.
> —Psalm 103:1–5

Open God's Word
to hear God's message

The mystery . . . has been kept hidden for ages and generations, but is now disclosed to the Lord's people. To them God has chosen to make known among the Gentiles the glorious riches of this mystery, which is Christ in you, the hope of glory.

—COLOSSIANS 1:26–27

Open Your Mind
to understand God's message then and now

You need more. That seems to be the message the Colossians were hearing from false teachers. You need to buy into the secret knowledge we give you. You need to follow our rules. You need to worship the angels we tell you about. Christ is fine for starters, but if you want the full experience, you need more.

That's bunk, said the apostle Paul in no uncertain terms. What you have in Jesus is better than anything those false teachers are promising. You want some secret knowledge? Well, here is the mystery of the ages clearly spelled out: Christ living in you, bringing you into a relationship with our glorious God.

Even today people will try to sell you on secret systems to make you holier or happier. If you only do this, pray this, or believe this, you will unlock the treasures of the universe. Beware of these spiels. Watch out for anything that shoves Jesus aside. He is sufficient. What you already have—Christ in you—is better than anything they're offering. It might sound like a good idea to try to improve your standing with God, but the only secret you need is Christ in you.

Open Your Heart
to the divine whisper

Relax in the wonder of this mystery: the Lord of all, Jesus Christ, lives within you. The One in whom "all things consist" (Colossians 1:17, NKJV) cares deeply about you. How does this make you feel?

_____

_____

_____

_____

_____

_____

_____

Open Your Life
to God's transforming power

It's easy for us to put the focus on ourselves. This can happen when we are acting out of pride and also out of humility. Most of us recognize the danger of exalting ourselves, as if we can impress God with our actions. But some folks worry that they haven't done enough to receive God's love. This can make you easy prey for the huckster's pitch: *If only you do this, this, and this, you'll find what you're missing.* And suddenly it's all about you, what *you* do. You're not focused on the Lord.

If that's your story, the answer is not to think more or less highly of yourself but to let God be God. Receive the grace He gives you. Welcome Christ into your life. Let His Spirit transform you according to His purposes. Work with Him as He does His work in you.

_____

_____

_____

_____

_____

_____

Open Your Arms
to a world that needs to receive God's incarnate message through you

For some people you may be the only Jesus they ever see. There was a time when our culture had a general knowledge of Christianity, but that's not true anymore. Some know "Jesus Christ" only as an exclamation. Some see Christians as hypocrites and haters. But since Christ is living in you, you have the opportunity to show others who He really is.

That probably won't mean preaching to people. But it definitely will mean loving them. And of course that includes caring for people's spiritual needs as well as their physical needs. So tell them the truth about Jesus, but also live in the truth of the glorious Savior, who's living in you.

What people in your world need to see Christ in you? What will this look like?

_____

_____

_____

_____

_____

_____

Open Yourself
to a dynamic encounter with God

Will you allow the Lord to change you today? Your thinking, your seeing, your long-held assumptions? Your habits, your relationships, your priorities? Your definitions of what it means to be human, to be good, to be a Christian? How will you allow Him to change you today?

Open God's Word
to hear God's message

You are no longer foreigners and strangers, but fellow citizens with God's people and also members of his household, built on the foundation of the apostles and prophets, with Christ Jesus himself as the chief cornerstone. In him the whole building is joined together and rises to become a holy temple in the Lord.

—EPHESIANS 2:19–21

Open Your Mind
to understand God's message then and now

This wasn't just a church Paul was writing to. The Ephesians were a social experiment.

On Paul's first preaching trip to that city, he was rejected by the synagogue for his dangerous ideas about the Messiah, and he set up shop at a lecture hall, where his message attracted both Jews and

Gentiles. This was groundbreaking. Jews had been taught not to associate with heathen Gentiles, who often responded badly to that exclusive attitude. Now they were worshiping together? How would that work?

In today's verses Paul describes a building under construction. It's the church, and the building blocks are people. Jews and Gentiles support each other in this construction, interlocking and rising higher. The cornerstone, of course, is Jesus, flanked by the teaching of ancient prophets and modern apostles—the prophets revered by Jews and the apostles now reaching out to the Gentiles.

Sociologists tell us that most people naturally get together with others who are just like them, and some local churches seem to reflect that principle. But while that may be a natural tendency, we must never forget that God's church is *super*natural. He brings people together from different races, languages, cultures, and religious backgrounds. In this new community we are "no longer foreigners and strangers, but fellow citizens."

Open Your Heart
to the divine whisper

Open my heart, Lord, to people who aren't *just like me. Let Your love move me to cross boundaries.*

What boundaries are you dealing with? How is God moving you?

_____

_____

_____

_____

_____

_____

Open Your Life
to God's transforming power

We put up walls even when we don't intend to. We avoid certain communities, certain groups, certain people. It's not that they're bad; they're just different. We feel uncomfortable around them. It's far easier to hang out with the people who understand us, who share our priorities and culture. Nothing wrong with that, is there?

Well, maybe we should consider how Jesus lived. He was a rabbi who feasted with prostitutes and tax collectors. He traveled through Samaria rather than bypassing it, as many other Jews did. He told a story with a Samaritan as a hero. He touched lepers. He welcomed children. And, as Paul put it, Jesus "destroyed the barrier, the dividing wall of hostility" (Ephesians 2:14).

Jesus broke down social walls in order to build a new, open structure. What walls need to come crashing down in your heart?

_____

_____

_____

_____

_____

_____

Open Your Arms
to a world that needs to receive God's incarnate message through you

Quiet your heart and listen for the Lord's guidance on the following matter. There's nothing here that's trendy or politically correct. Whatever you do needs to be prompted by God.

Let Him bring to mind some group of people you have avoided, rejected, or suspected. It could be a language or cultural group, a race or nationality, those of a particular religious background, or even an age or gender—any group of people you have a walled off from your concern.

How does the Lord feel about the way you have treated these people? More important, what does He want you to do now? Is there a way to make contact, to reach across the boundary, to start dismantling the wall? Listen. God will give you an idea. Make it a matter of continual prayer—and action.

_____

_____

_____

_____

_____

_____

_____

Open Yourself
to a dynamic encounter with God

You might want to think of this regular time with the Lord as a recharge, plugging into a power source. How will it energize you today?

Open God's Word
to hear God's message

And if the Spirit of him who raised Jesus from the dead is living in you, he who raised Christ from the dead will also give life to your mortal bodies because of his Spirit who lives in you.

—ROMANS 8:11

Open Your Mind
to understand God's message then and now

How can we be righteous in God's eyes and in our earthly lives? That's the through-line of the book of Romans. In lawyerly fashion Paul lays out his argument: we are sinners who deserve the death penalty; our only hope is to trust in Christ; He has paid that penalty for us; in His death, we die.

Here in Romans 8 the apostle takes an exciting new step. Not only does Jesus's death pay for our sins, but His resurrection raises us to a new kind of life. God's Spirit lives within us, guiding us, comforting us, and empowering us. This is, after all, the Spirit who raised Jesus from the dead.

The results are profound. We are "called according to his purpose" (8:28). We are "more than conquerors" over a host of spiritual challenges (8:37). We are a "living sacrifice"—not one-and-done on the altar but stepping up each day to serve God (12:1). Our thought processes are "transformed" and renewed (see 12:2).

This is the resurrection life shared by all who trust Christ.

Open Your Heart
to the divine whisper

Thank God for the miracle of resurrection: the raising of Christ and the empowering of *you*.

What does resurrection life look like as you live it? Let the Spirit bring you images of what it could be. What do you see?

_____

_____

_____

_____

_____

_____

Open Your Life
to God's transforming power

Do you really want to be resurrected? Do you really want the life that God's Spirit is giving you? That might seem like a silly question, but we often get lulled into complacency. We become like zombies, the walking dead. We sing the songs on Sundays and say the prayers, but then we trudge from day to day, paycheck to paycheck, bill to bill, with little energy or purpose.

Don't you want more *life* in your life? Won't you join God's Spirit on a thrill ride? Can't you get off the couch, veer out of the commuter lane, step forward in faith, and explore some uncharted territory? Breathe in the life of the Spirit and follow where He leads.

Where might He be leading you?

_____

_____

_____

_____

_____

_____

Open Your Arms
to a world that needs to receive God's incarnate message through you

Our culture breeds death—from gang violence to abortion clinics, from human trafficking to pornography, from anorexic waifs starving themselves to be beautiful to steroid-stoking athletes poisoning themselves to be victorious. We routinely trade life-giving relationships for the monotony of game screens. We watch death happen every day on television crime shows, and nonstop news networks repeat the grisly details of each deadly disaster until we're numb to it.

What can you do to bring life to the world rather than death?

As Christians, we don't just *have* a life-giving message to share with the world; we *are* a life-giving message to share with the world. The Spirit has given us new life. What are we going to do with it?

Here are a few suggestions. There are great organizations devoted to easing the starvation of the world. There are also organizations that fight the deadening effects of enslavement in various forms—human trafficking, prostitution, and addiction. Other ministries address the spiritual enslavement of people with the freeing message of Christ. Can you connect meaningfully with one of these?

Please understand: we're not trying to guilt you into writing a check to a charity. This is about sharing your resurrection life with others who desperately need it.

Is the Lord leading you to get involved in a life-giving ministry?

_____

_____

_____

_____

_____

_____

Open Yourself
to a dynamic encounter with God

As you approach this time with the Lord today, imagine yourself as a tablet of paper with a blank page on top. (Or if you are more computer-minded, you're a blank screen.) What message will the Spirit write on your heart today?

Open God's Word
to hear God's message

Do we need, like some people, letters of recommendation to you or from you? You yourselves are our letter, written on our hearts, known and read by everyone. You show that you are a letter from Christ, the result of our ministry, written not with ink but with the Spirit of the living God, not on tablets of stone but on tablets of human hearts.

—2 CORINTHIANS 3:1–3

Open Your Mind
to understand God's message then and now

Apparently the Corinthians were dealing with a swarm of teachers flashing their diplomas and boasting about their own speaking ability. They loved telling everyone how unqualified Paul was. *Why doesn't that so-called apostle show us his credentials?*

Paul responds here, in essence, "*You* are my credentials." The lives of the Corinthian Christians proved the validity of the gospel Paul taught. His résumé could match anyone else's, but he didn't choose to play that game. Ultimately no letter of recommendation was necessary. The people themselves were that letter.

This leads to a fascinating comparison. This letter is not carved in stone but inscribed with God's Spirit upon the human heart. That makes a big difference. Stone is dead; the heart is alive. Later Paul talks about how the Law, inscribed on tablets of stone, is deadly, but God's Spirit brings life (see verses 6–7).

It would seem, then, that our lives prove the gospel *not* by how carefully we follow the rules but by how fully we follow the Spirit's guidance. The Lord's desires get embossed on our hearts. We learn to want what He wants.

Open Your Heart
to the divine whisper

In the silence consider the Spirit's calligraphy in your life. What masterpiece is He penning?

_____

_____

_____

_____

Open Your Life
to God's transforming power

There are few scriptures that convey the "be the message" idea as clearly as this one. The truth of Paul's preaching was confirmed by the lives of the believers in Corinth. This is especially interesting when we consider that the Corinthians were the problem children of Paul's ministry. He spent most of his first epistle to them troubleshooting, and they had lots of troubles: factions, discrimination against the poor, a sex scandal, chaotic worship services, and lawsuits, to name a few. These people were far from perfect, and still the apostle considered them his "letters of recommendation."

So maybe our public testimony is based less on our own righteousness and more on the reality of God in our lives. The message that we embody is not "Look at us! We're perfect!" It's "See the amazing things God can do in the lives of imperfect people!"

Your life will be a mixture of trial and error, success and failure, thanksgiving and confession. Through it all, the Spirit of God is writing His grace on your heart. Yes, your behavior matters. You always want to live in a way that pleases and praises Him. But your mistakes, when they happen, do not invalidate the message. They just allow you to flip to the chapter on forgiveness.

Many of us try to hide from God when we mess up, and we hide our sins from others. But the gospel of grace is a message of honesty and redemption. It is not based on our perfection but on His love.

In light of this, what kind of honest conversation do you need to have with God?

_____

_____

_____

_____

_____

Open Your Arms
to a world that needs to receive God's incarnate message through you

Think of the people who have influenced your faith just as Paul influenced the Corinthians. Teachers, preachers, parents, friends. You are their "letters of recommendation."

Also, think of those *you* have influenced. Have you nurtured some in their Christian commitment?

As these names and faces drift through your mind, let God lead you to one of them who could really use a message of support right now. Then send this person that message. An e-mail or phone call would suffice, but maybe you could surprise her with a good old-fashioned letter. Quote today's verse if you like, but let her know how special she is.

Whom will you contact? What will you say?

_____

_____

_____

_____

_____

_____

Open Yourself
to a dynamic encounter with God

> Because of the LORD's great love we are not consumed,
>> for his compassions never fail.
> They are new every morning;
>> great is your faithfulness.
> —Lamentations 3:22–23

This was written in a time of great pain, and yet the prophet found hope. As you come to the Lord today, can you put aside your personal pain and focus on God's faithfulness?

Open God's Word
to hear God's message

You intended to harm me, but God intended it for good to accomplish what is now being done, the saving of many lives.

—GENESIS 50:20

Open Your Mind
to understand God's message then and now

Today's verse is a satisfying postscript to an epic Bible story. It is uttered by Joseph to the brothers who had sold him into slavery decades earlier.

You may remember how it goes. Joseph, the favorite son of his father, Jacob, is grabbed by his jealous brothers and traded to a passing caravan headed for Egypt. There he serves well in a household until he is falsely accused of rape. Then he becomes a model prisoner, known for interpreting dreams. It just so happens that Pharaoh, the king of Egypt, has a troubling dream that needs interpretation. Joseph wows Pharaoh and becomes the country's prime minister, administering an ambitious program of famine relief. That's when his brothers show up, needing food. After toying with them a bit, Joseph feels he can trust them enough to reveal his identity. There's a tearful reunion.

But Joseph makes this statement sometime later. After Jacob dies, the brothers worry that Joseph will finally take revenge. With this statement he assures them that he bears no grudge. God had a higher purpose all along.

Open Your Heart
to the divine whisper

God may ask you today to deal with some things you've repressed for a long time. Are you ready for that? If you've been mistreated in the past and you're still stewing over it, He may be showing you a way to get past it. Talk with Him about this—and listen.

_____

_____

_____

_____

_____

_____

_____

Open Your Life
to God's transforming power

Joseph's statement is remarkable in its simplicity, honesty, and maturity. He does not excuse or downplay his brothers' sin. They had indeed tried to hurt him. Sometimes we get the idea that forgiveness means shrugging off an injury. "No problem!" we say, but of course it is a problem. False forgiveness doesn't really help. True forgiveness faces the sin squarely and chooses not to hate the sinner.

We also find here a stunning expression of how God transforms bad situations. According to His purposes, He regularly works things together for an ultimate good. This is not to say that Joseph's brothers were off the hook for their misdeeds just because God transformed a bad situation into a good one. Same with anyone who has hurt you. It just means that God is not stymied by people's bad behavior. His plans prevail. And in His awesome creativity, He seems to create new plans that redeem the pain of the past.

How has God redeemed bad situations in your life?

_____

_____

_____

_____

_____

Open Your Arms
to a world that needs to receive God's incarnate message through you

When we hang on to past pain, it usually hurts us more than anyone else. Joseph apparently greeted each new challenge with a fresh spirit. We don't see him sulking or grumbling as a slave or prisoner; instead, he keeps succeeding in these difficult circumstances.

Have you been holding grudges? Do you find it hard to let go of the pain others have caused you? How has this affected your attitude, your relationships, your spiritual life? Take some time now to pour out these situations before the Lord. See what He has to say about them. What does He want to transform?

Forgiveness is seldom easy, especially if you're dealing with long-held hurts. But God might lead you to take a step toward the renewal of a broken relationship. How and with whom might that step occur?

_____

_____

_____

_____

_____

_____

Open Yourself
to a dynamic encounter with God

Some of the psalms have a refrain that's frequently repeated. "Give thanks to the LORD, for he is good. *His love endures forever*" (Psalm 136, for example). As you come before the Lord today, repeat this glorious truth: *Your love endures forever*.

Open God's Word
to hear God's message

All praise to the God and Father of our Master, Jesus the Messiah! Father of all mercy! God of all healing counsel! He comes alongside us when we go through hard times, and before you know it, he brings us alongside someone else who is going through hard times so that we can be there for that person just as God was there for us.

—2 CORINTHIANS 1:3–4, MSG

Open Your Mind
to understand God's message then and now

The apostle had written frankly and harshly in his first letter to the Corinthians, who had a lot of issues to deal with. But here at the beginning of the second letter, he takes a new tone: *comfort*. He assures them that God still loves them and can still use them for His glory. All of us, he says, are just "jars of clay" (4:7), holding God's glory in our earthen selves. But God is still re-creating us, making us new, and sending us out as His peace envoys, seeking reconciliation with a troubled world.

That new tone of comfort starts in these verses with a delightful two-step. God comforts us so we can comfort others. The Message digs to the root of the *comfort* verb—to come alongside. It's a friend putting an arm around your shoulders and walking with you. This is the same word Jesus used for the Holy Spirit, often translated Comforter, Counselor, Helper, or Guide but literally "one who is called alongside."

That in itself inspires a response of thanks and praise, but there's more. After we receive comfort from God, we are prepared to give it to others. If you're a parent, mentor, or coach, perhaps you've given some encouraging words to a child and suddenly realized these were the exact same words you once received from your parents, mentors, or coaches. That's the way it works. We give what we get.

People in need walk beside us every day. Our own struggles don't disqualify us from helping them. On the contrary, we are uniquely equipped to provide God's comfort.

Open Your Heart
to the divine whisper

Imagine the Lord beside you, putting a comforting arm around your shoulder. Take some time just to feel His presence close to you. What is He whispering in your ear?

_____

_____

_____

_____

_____

Open Your Life
to God's transforming power

Perhaps you've been searching for a reason for your suffering. Sickness, tragedy, a broken relationship, a dashed dream . . . *Why, God, why?* Many people of faith have pounded on heaven's door with that question.

Here's one answer. It doesn't make everything all better, but it might help. *God is equipping you to help others.* Because of what you're going through and how God is comforting you, you have a certain expertise. You can now put your arm around someone else, because you've been there.

We see this often in life. An old soldier haunted by battlefield trauma needs the support of another vet, not some coddled academic. An alcoholic finds accountability with a sponsor who has shared the same struggle. And whatever trial you've been through puts you in a unique position to help others. Consider the comfort God has given you, and share that with others.

What have you learned from God's comforting skills?

_____

_____

_____

_____

_____

Open Your Arms
to a world that needs to receive God's incarnate message through you

Try to learn this two-step. First, think of the times when you have received comfort and help from the Lord. What have you struggled with? How has He helped you? Take time to let these memories—however painful—return.

Are you troubled by these memories, perhaps embarrassed? Do you want to hide them or run from them? On the basis of today's verse, we can say that God has a different plan in mind.

Let Him bring to your mind and heart images of people who are now facing similar struggles—neighbors, coworkers, relatives, friends at church. Maybe they hide their struggle, but you've been there; you know it's happening. Focus on one of these images, one person who needs someone to come alongside.

What will you do or say to offer God's comfort to that person?

_____

_____

_____

_____

_____

_____

Open Yourself
to a dynamic encounter with God

The Lord is with you always, but this is a time you set aside to be with Him. Remove the distractions as best you can, and focus on Him. How will He grow your soul today?

Open God's Word
to hear God's message

Be strong and courageous, because you will lead these people to inherit the land I swore to their ancestors to give them.

Be strong and very courageous. Be careful to obey all the law my servant Moses gave you; do not turn from it to the right or to the left, that you may be successful wherever you go. Keep this Book of the Law always on your lips; meditate on it day and night, so that you may be careful to do everything written in it. Then you will be prosperous and successful. Have I not commanded you? Be strong and courageous. Do not be afraid; do not be discouraged, for the LORD your God will be with you wherever you go.

—JOSHUA 1:6–9

Open Your Mind
to understand God's message then and now

Moses was larger than life.

Nearly all the Israelites who had left Egypt had died in the wilderness, and a new generation had grown up who knew no other leader. Moses was the one who had raised his staff and parted the Red Sea. He had looked God in the eye and lived to tell about it, his face shining like the sun. He had received the Law on Mount Sinai.

And now he was dead. What would happen now?

Joshua had been groomed for this moment "since youth" (Numbers 11:28). A trusted military commander, he had been with Moses at Sinai. He had scouted out the Promised Land and recommended an invasion, only to be overruled by the majority. He had been chosen and consecrated as Moses's successor.

Still, it had to be a scary moment. We know this because God said to him *repeatedly,* "Be strong and courageous." (Joshua had also heard this several times *before* Moses died.) Even the best-prepared leaders need encouragement.

Indeed, Joshua proved to be a strong leader, as the rest of the book of Joshua bears out. He led the Israelites into the Promised Land, oversaw their settlement, and provided some crucial spiritual guidance shortly before his own death, challenging the people to *choose* to serve the Lord God.

Open Your Heart
to the divine whisper

Hear the Lord's voice in your heart repeating, "Be strong and courageous." What is He telling you about how and where to display that courage?

_____

_____

_____

_____

_____

_____

_____

Open Your Life
to God's transforming power

Sometimes humble people have trouble being strong and courageous. We are thoroughly aware of our own limitations. We know we don't have the leadership skills of Moses or even Joshua. We're not going to command an army or explore new territory. We're just going to grind through each day. Not a lot of courage needed for that, is there?

The truth is, we don't know what we'll need strength and courage for. The daily grind holds lots of surprises, lots of challenges. A coworker who needs emotional support. A neighbor who needs prayer. Kids who need guidance. Aging parents who need a new place to live. You might be more of a leader than you think, and you'll need all the strength and courage you can get.

So *how* can we be strong and courageous, especially when we're completely incapable of the tasks at hand? Today's passage provides a fascinating progression. First, it tells us to follow God's Word. To be a good servant, obey. Then it says to connect with what God says. Meditate on it, repeat it. It needs to move from commandments chiseled in stone to convictions growing in our hearts. Finally, it reminds us that the Lord is always with us. Whenever we falter, He's beside us, picking us up, strengthening and encouraging us.

Stop focusing on what you can't do. Focus on what God can do through you.

_____

_____

_____

_____

Open Your Arms
to a world that needs to receive God's incarnate message through you

If you were to put aside your self-doubt and take Joshua's "strong and courageous" advice, what could happen?

Is there some new ministry needed at your church? Or does God want you to start a prayer group at your business? Can you find more effective ways to help the poor in your community? Or maybe you just need to get to know the neighbors you've been driving past for the last decade. Is God filling your heart with concern for those in a particular place? Are you especially concerned about hunger, education, trafficking, or homelessness?

How is God prompting you? "Be strong and courageous" enough to follow through on these promptings.

_____

_____

_____

_____

Open Yourself
to a dynamic encounter with God

How are you feeling today, really? Bring God your praises but also your pains, your faith, and your frustration. Lay it all out before the Lord. He wants to work with it.

Open God's Word
to hear God's message

Moreover we know that to those who love God, who are called according to his plan, everything that happens fits into a pattern for good.

—ROMANS 8:28, PHILLIPS

Open Your Mind
to understand God's message then and now

Synergy. It has become a buzzword in modern business. It's when different parts of a company or project fit together like a well-oiled machine, everything working in a smooth flow. The results are good, far better than you'd expect from the individual parts of the process.

That's exactly the word used in Romans 8:28, a well-known verse that's extremely comforting but often misunderstood. Some versions say all things *work together* (*synergei,* in Greek) for good. We've used the Phillips translation here because it's less susceptible to misunderstanding. The verse does not say everything that happens to us *is* good, nor does it say that everything will turn out pleasantly for us.

For those who love God, who have a calling to fulfill God's plans, God will work things out according to His good purposes.

This is very much like Joseph's announcement to his brothers in Genesis 50:20. They had tried to hurt him, but God had repurposed their actions to accomplish something very good—the saving of many lives. In the same way, we will have to suffer from time to time, but through it all, God is working for His good purposes. There is a synergy between God and us and even the bad things that befall us.

The key to Romans 8:28 may be in verse 29, which speaks of our conforming to the image of Jesus. This is God's purpose for us, to make us ever more like Christ. Did Jesus have to suffer? Absolutely. In order to accomplish a greater purpose—the saving of many lives.

Open Your Heart
to the divine whisper

Thank God for His synergy, for working with all the elements of your life to accomplish His purposes. You probably have no idea how He's going to do that. That's okay. Ask Him your questions and listen for His answers. What are His plans for you? Are you willing to let Him use your painful experiences for a greater good?

_____

_____

_____

_____

_____

_____

_____

Open Your Life
to God's transforming power

All of us want an easy life, right? We want to be happy, healthy, and financially solvent. We want good relationships and meaningful work. There's nothing wrong with wanting things to go well for us.

But what happens when they don't? You get injured, and insurance doesn't cover it. Your kid rebels. Your neighbor slanders you. Your company moves to a foreign country without you. A good friend dies far too young. Any number of things can suddenly make life difficult. How do you react when they do?

Many of us feel gypped. We accuse God of falling down on the job. How could He let this happen to us? We assume that easy is normal and difficult is just wrong. Doesn't God owe us a good life as long as we're faithful to Him?

No. The consistent teaching of Scripture is that God doesn't owe us anything. It's normal to face trouble. That doesn't mean God is punishing or rejecting us. In fact, it can give us a chance to trust Him even more. Every barrier that arises to block us from "the good life" can become a bridge to a better life—measured not in terms of money or physical pleasure but in our intimacy with God.

God transforms our difficult situations not by making everything easy again but by nurturing us through the pain and helping us to conform to the image of Christ.

How do you feel God is transforming your difficulties?

_____

_____

_____

_____

_____

_____

_____

Open Your Arms
to a world that needs to receive God's incarnate message through you

Let God bring to your mind someone who is dealing with a painful situation—illness, injury, divorce, unemployment, bereavement . . .

Can you make contact with this person and simply be the message of God to him? Avoid judgment or even analysis. The message is all about God's love and support in this difficult time. You don't need to say the perfect thing that will make everything all better. You can't. In fact, you might not even have to say a word. Just be there with him as our Immanuel is with us.

Whom will you connect with, and how will you do it?

_____

_____

_____

_____

_____

_____

Open Yourself
to a dynamic encounter with God

> Show me the way I should go,
>   for to you I entrust my life.
>   —Psalm 143:8

Open God's Word
to hear God's message

Therefore, in order to keep me from becoming conceited, I was given a thorn in my flesh, a messenger of Satan, to torment me. Three times I pleaded with the Lord to take it away from me. But he said to me, "My grace is sufficient for you, for my power is made perfect in weakness." Therefore I will boast all the more gladly about my weaknesses, so that Christ's power may rest on me. That is why, for Christ's sake, I delight in weaknesses, in insults, in hardships, in persecutions, in difficulties. For when I am weak, then I am strong.

—2 CORINTHIANS 12:7–10

Open Your Mind
to understand God's message then and now

It's one of the great mysteries of the Bible. *What was Paul's "thorn in the flesh"?* Some say it was an eye problem, perhaps a holdover from being temporarily blinded on the Damascus Road. Others suggest epilepsy, depression, or even migraine headaches.

Whatever the official diagnosis, it was a big problem for the apostle, and he prayed to be rid of it. Three times he prayed, and God said no. Well, God said more than just "No!" In the verses we focus on today, the Lord gave Paul—and us—a beautiful reminder of His grace and power.

His grace is all we need. His power finds its completion in our weakness.

This was a game changer for Paul. Suddenly his life was about more than being the smartest guy in the room. He didn't have to be the best preacher ever. The debilitating effects of this "thorn," whatever it was, forced him to rely on the grace of God. Whatever Paul had to offer was what God offered *him*. His weakness would demonstrate God's strength.

Open Your Heart
to the divine whisper

Consider those personal issues you've been praying about, and bring them before the Lord right now. (Note that He never scolded Paul for praying about his thorn in the flesh.) This time, however, instead of begging God to remove the problem, see what grace He wants to show you.

_____

_____

_____

_____

_____

_____

Open Your Life
to God's transforming power

The world's zest for success easily creeps into Christian conversation. We want to be the best disciples we can be, rising victorious over life's problems, moving mountainous obstacles with our strong faith, attempting great things for God, and expecting Him to come through. Super Christians.

Except we're not that, and we don't have to be.

There's certainly nothing wrong with discipleship, victory, faith, or risk. But it's not about us. Paul's "thorn in the flesh" experience teaches us that the best quality we bring to God is our weakness. He does the rest.

Faith moves mountains not because we believe so strongly but because we trust in a strong God. In fact, there's something a bit contradictory in the term "strong faith." Our faith is strongest when we admit our weakness and rely fully on God.

What is God telling you about this?

_____

_____

_____

_____

_____

_____

Open Your Arms
to a world that needs to receive God's incarnate message through you

There may be someone in your orbit who has had a bad experience with Super Christians. As a result, she may have turned away from God.

We don't need to spend too much time knocking these overzealous believers. They're trying to be good Christians. But somewhere along the way, the emphasis shifted from Christ to their own goodness or rightness, and people got hurt.

How can you, in all your weakness, reach out and help the wounded ones? You don't need to have all the answers. In fact, that would probably make things worse. You may fear that you lack evangelistic skills. You're worried that you'll do or say something wrong. Relax. You're working from God's strength, not your own.

All you have to offer is God's grace, but that is enough. How can you be the message of divine grace in this situation?

_____

_____

_____

_____

_____

_____

Open Yourself
to a dynamic encounter with God

Think of this as a meal you're sharing with Jesus. Chat with Him as freely as you would with a brunch companion.

Open God's Word
to hear God's message

While Jesus was having dinner at Matthew's house, many tax collectors and sinners came and ate with him and his disciples. When the Pharisees saw this, they asked his disciples, "Why does your teacher eat with tax collectors and sinners?"

On hearing this, Jesus said, "It is not the healthy who need a doctor, but the sick. But go and learn what this means: 'I desire mercy, not sacrifice.' For I have not come to call the righteous, but sinners."

—MATTHEW 9:10–13

Open Your Mind
to understand God's message then and now

Jesus feasted with sinners. He still does.

In New Testament times there was a whole class of people who weren't even trying to follow God's Law. So as the Pharisees attempted to make the whole nation righteous, they wrote off this group as sinners. *Surely God won't expect us to turn those people around.*

Of course they were shocked and horrified when Jesus began

feasting with such people. He even selected a tax collector, Matthew, as one of His disciples. And we haven't even mentioned the prostitutes. How could a respected rabbi associate with the moral dregs of society?

Jesus's answer was witty and somewhat ironic. Doesn't a doctor need to associate with sick people? The irony comes from the fact that the Pharisees weren't as healthy as they thought. Jesus urged them to "learn" a verse from the prophet Hosea, stating that God prefers mercy over religious ritual (6:6). The Pharisees got high marks in ritual, but they were sorely deficient in showing mercy (as seen in their rejection of those sinners).

Tax collectors and prostitutes knew they couldn't save themselves, and many came to Jesus for the cure. The Pharisees mistakenly thought they themselves were just fine.

Open Your Heart
to the divine whisper

Take a few minutes in the silence to mull over today's scripture. Put yourself in that scene, as a Pharisee, as a sinner, as one of Jesus's disciples. Consider the different angles.

What do you see?

_____

_____

_____

_____

_____

_____

_____

_____

Open Your Life
to God's transforming power

Here's one subtle shift between the two Testaments. In the Old Testament, impurity was contagious. The Israelites were warned about touching unclean things: blood, dead bodies, lepers. This made sense as a health regulation, but it carried over into the moral code. Jews were not to dine with Gentiles, for instance, because they were "unclean."

Jesus took a very different approach: touching lepers, allowing a bleeding woman to touch Him, and dining with sinners. In His view, apparently, *grace* was contagious. He would not be tainted by contact with impure people, but He might bring purity to them. The New Testament church expanded into the Gentile world on this notion.

How do you feel about this today? Are you worried about being contaminated by the moral filth of the world? That's a reasonable concern, but should it block us from following Jesus's call to minister to needy souls?

What is God telling you about that?

_____

_____

_____

_____

_____

Open Your Arms
to a world that needs to receive God's incarnate message through you

We offer two different suggestions for two different situations.

The first suggestion is for those who have shut themselves off from meaningful contact with unbelievers. You spend most of your time doing Christian things with Christian people, and God blesses you greatly. But could you reach out of your Christian world to establish a friendship with someone who doesn't know Christ? Could you join a community theater, book club, or bowling team as a way of doing what Jesus did—feasting with sinners?

The second suggestion is for Christians who already have meaningful friendships with unbelievers. Consider how you can be the message in those relationships. You don't need to preach or harangue, but can you bring Jesus into those encounters?

We want to affect the world more than we're affected by it. And, you know, this world talks freely about anything and everything. People openly share intimate details of the lives of celebrities—their latest breakup, their mug shot on a drunk-driving arrest, or the doctor who did their plastic surgery. Why can't we talk about Jesus, the Doctor who has healed us?

Will you take one of these suggestions? If so, how? With whom?

_____

_____

_____

_____

_____

Open Yourself
to a dynamic encounter with God

As you settle into this encounter, take a few deep breaths. Imagine the Spirit of God filling you as you inhale and moving outward to bless others as you exhale.

Open God's Word
to hear God's message

But you will receive power when the Holy Spirit comes on you; and you will be my witnesses in Jerusalem, and in all Judea and Samaria, and to the ends of the earth.

—ACTS 1:8

Open Your Mind
to understand God's message then and now

In the gospels we get different versions of what we call the Great Commission, suggesting that Jesus repeated this teaching at points during the forty days after His resurrection. This version in Acts has some unique qualities arising from the disciples' question about the future of Israel. Jesus answered, essentially, "I can't tell you that, but here's what I know about *your* future."

Power. The Holy Spirit. They would be witnesses.

What a great word! A witness experiences something and tells about it in court or on the news. A witness doesn't make up stories or sell an idea or preach. A witness just tells the truth. And note that Jesus said "my witnesses." They would be vouching for Jesus.

In Jerusalem, Judea, Samaria, and the ends of the earth. The pebble tossed in a pond in Jerusalem rippled outward, through the region of Judea, to the neighboring (and hostile) country of Samaria, and to the mysterious lands beyond.

This is exactly what happened. The message rippled outward to the whole world.

Open Your Heart
to the divine whisper

In this time of reflection, consider your experience with Jesus. If a witness is someone who experiences something and tells about it, what do you have to talk about?

_____

_____

_____

_____

Open Your Life
to God's transforming power

Are you expecting a guilt trip right now? *You should do more witnessing!* Relax. Whatever we do with this verse, it comes from the power of the Holy Spirit, not our own communication skills.

So how will we be witnesses? We simply tell the truth about our experience with Jesus. This is actually quite close to the "be the message" theme we've been developing. There's no manufacturing necessary, no manipulation. We simply say what we know. We are who we are. We live the reality of a risen Jesus.

It might be more helpful to consider the *where* of this verse. Where do those ripples carry us? *Jerusalem* is where you are—your hometown, maybe just your home. The people closest to you will see what's happening in your life. You will be a message to them, whether or not you try to be.

With *Judea* our vision starts to lift to the surrounding region. How will your message get out there?

The inclusion of *Samaria* is especially interesting. It was geographically close but socially distant. Samaritans were despised by the Jews for political and religious reasons. To be a witness in Samaria meant crossing social boundaries, entering dangerous territory. Where is your Samaria? Another culture? A people group you try to avoid? A different religion? A competing political persuasion?

For the Jews standing around Jesus, *the ends of the earth* meant Gentile territory. This was even more mysterious and far more ambitious. How would these disciples even get to those places? Long journeys by foot, beast, and boat. This would be a commitment of major proportions.

How will you be this witness/message in your world? What places and people will God bring into your heart?

_____

_____

_____

_____

Open Your Arms
to a world that needs to receive God's incarnate message through you

Paul once dreamed of a faraway person calling, "Come over . . . and help us" (Acts 16:9). At the time he had gone as far as he had planned to go. He was about to head back, but then this vision beckoned him farther.

When we talk about opening your arms to the person right in front of you, that could be a faraway person whom God is putting right in front of you in your thoughts, dreams, or prayers.

Stop thinking of boundaries. God can lead you beyond them. Your hometown or home church needs you, sure, but maybe God needs you somewhere else, to be His message in a distant land within a difficult culture.

Here's what you can do now: Listen more for God's calling. Keep your heart and mind open for His surprising direction.

Study the place or people God is talking to you about.

Talk with a mature believer. Get some wise feedback on your calling.

Connect with people who are currently ministering in that area.

Consider a short-term mission opportunity.

What is God telling you now about the possibilities?

_____

_____

_____

_____

_____

Open Yourself
to a dynamic encounter with God

As you come to this special time with God, what's distracting you? Are there worries or obligations demanding your attention? Intentionally put them aside. Devote this time to the Lord.

Open God's Word
to hear God's message

A certain ruler asked him, "Good teacher, what must I do to inherit eternal life?"

"Why do you call me good?" Jesus answered. "No one is good—except God alone. You know the commandments: 'You shall not commit adultery, you shall not murder, you shall not steal, you shall not give false testimony, honor your father and mother.'"

"All these I have kept since I was a boy," he said.

When Jesus heard this, he said to him, "You still lack one thing. Sell everything you have and give to the poor, and you will have treasure in heaven. Then come, follow me."

When he heard this, he became very sad, because he was very wealthy.

—LUKE 18:18–23

Open Your Mind
to understand God's message then and now

We don't know his name. We just call him the rich young ruler as we gather clues about him from the different gospel accounts. *Ruler* probably means he was a leader in the local synagogue. As a young man, he was apparently succeeding at everything, including religion.

He sidles up to Jesus and asks for the secret of eternal life. Jesus once told a story of a rich fool who amassed his wealth with no thought for eternity (see Luke 12:13–21). The rich young ruler has more awareness than that. He's asking the right question, and he's asking the right rabbi.

We might quibble with his assumption that he has to earn eternal life, but it's no surprise that a businessman would think in those terms. Note that Jesus does not correct him on this point. He just confirms that the man is genuinely keeping the commandments and then, oh, God requires one more thing.

Everything.

Suddenly the man isn't as devout as he thinks he is. To give away everything would mean complete dependence on God. Where would he live? How would he eat? Would he lose his place in society?

It may be the saddest scene in Scripture, the slumping shoulders of the man who walks away from Jesus because he owns too much stuff.

Open Your Heart
to the divine whisper

Review that scene from the perspective of the rich man. What was Jesus demanding? Talk with the Lord about what He might want from you.

_____

_____

_____

_____

_____

Open Your Life
to God's transforming power

We are far too quick to assure ourselves that Jesus doesn't want *all of us* to give up our possessions. You can't earn eternal life even with a massive donation to charity. Clearly Jesus knew that wealth was this man's idol, and He challenged him precisely on that point.

Whew! It's a good thing *we* don't worship money.

But of course we do. It's worth wondering how *we* would respond to the same challenge. If Jesus looked us in the eye and said, "Sell it all," would we?

Do our possessions hold us back from following Jesus? Are we chained to our stuff? This is not to say that money is bad or that no one should own anything, but the clear teaching of Scripture in several passages is that wealth easily becomes an idol. It's dangerous in that way. It's a trap. Money love is a root of all kinds of evil. You can't serve both God and money.

Through the ages a number of Christians have sold their houses, liquidated their assets, and entered a low-paying ministry. They have lived and served among the poor, sharing the eternal riches of Christ.

How do you feel about that? Is that something you could ever do? How devoted are you to your money? How does God feel about what you have, what you spend, and what you give? How does your relationship to wealth affect your relationship with God?

_____

_____

_____

_____

Open Your Arms
to a world that needs to receive God's incarnate message through you

The story of the rich young ruler is not all about money. It's about worship. That doesn't let any of us off the hook, however. The worship of money is prevalent in society and even in the church. We must be vigilant about this.

Routinely we make life decisions based on the bottom line. We assume that more money means a better life. But what if we stopped assuming that? What if we started talking with each other about the limits of money and the importance of nonmonetary blessings?

Is this any crazier than what Jesus told the rich young ruler? The message of Jesus is that God is far more important than money. How will you be that message?

_____

_____

_____

_____

Open Yourself
to a dynamic encounter with God

Pull yourself away from whatever battles you are fighting these days.
Call a truce and spend some peacetime here in the Lord's presence.

Open God's Word
to hear God's message

Listen, King Jehoshaphat and all who live in Judah and Jerusalem!
This is what the LORD says to you: "Do not be afraid or discouraged
because of this vast army. For the battle is not yours, but God's. . . .
You will not have to fight this battle. Take up your positions; stand
firm and see the deliverance the LORD will give you, Judah and Jerusalem. Do not be afraid; do not be discouraged. Go out to face them
tomorrow, and the LORD will be with you."

—2 CHRONICLES 20:15, 17

Open Your Mind
to understand God's message then and now

The ninth century BC was an in-between time. King Jehoshaphat
ruled Judah one hundred years after Solomon and one hundred years
before the brutal Assyrians began dominating the Mideast. Solomon's
glorious kingdom had split, north and south, and now both Israel and
Judah were scrapping with other small nations in the region.

This story concerns a threat from the nations on the eastern side of the Dead Sea—Ammon, Moab, and Edom. They were sending a combined force to fight Judah, and Jehoshaphat was mobilizing his troops for defense. The outlook was not good. The king offered, in public, a prayer of desperation, concluding, "We have no power to face this vast army that is attacking us. We do not know what to do, but our eyes are on you" (verse 12).

Then a prophet who had a curious message stood up. The Lord would fight this battle for them. They wouldn't have to lift a finger. Armed with that promise, the king called for musicians to lead the way to the battlefield as they sang God's praises: "Give thanks to the LORD, for his love endures forever" (verse 21).

Things turned out exactly as prophesied. The enemy forces had been killing each other, and when Judah's army showed up, there was no one left to fight. The praises continued on the way home.

Open Your Heart
to the divine whisper

What does it mean for the Lord to fight your battles? Which battles do you need to turn over to Him? How does that work? Talk with Him about all this.

_____

_____

_____

_____

_____

_____

Open Your Life
to God's transforming power

Old Testament stories like this, anchored in history, often hold spiritual meaning for us today. This one comes through loud and clear. We are strongest when we realize how weak we are and when we call on God for help. When we have no clue what to do, God has us right where He wants us. When we see that we are incapable of fighting our battles, He will fight for us.

We struggle to earn enough money. We scrape to get a new job. We worry about our kids. We strive to resist bad habits. And at a certain point, we give up. *I can't do this anymore. There's no way I can come out ahead. Lord, help!*

Can you hear His promise? "Do not be afraid or discouraged. . . . You will not have to fight this battle." He still asks us to show up, as Jehoshaphat did, to witness the miracle and sing His praises. The trusting life is not spent on the couch watching videos. We're *involved,* but the Lord is fighting for us. *He* wins the victory.

What struggles do you need to turn over to God? What will that look like in your life?

_____

_____

_____

_____

_____

_____

_____

Open Your Arms
to a world that needs to receive God's incarnate message through you

If you have been learning this lesson, it's a valuable one to share with others. Look around you for those who are overwhelmed, as if a massive army is arrayed against them. The hope you offer them is far more than positive thinking—"It's always darkest before the dawn." You have God's promise to offer them. If they trust Him, He will work powerfully in their situation.

Consider also how God can use *you* to make the situation less overwhelming. Is there some tangible assistance you could provide?

_____

_____

_____

_____

_____

_____

Open Yourself
to a dynamic encounter with God

As you begin this time with the Lord, picture His light beaming down from heaven and filling you. See that light shining out and affecting the lives of others in various ways.

Open God's Word
to hear God's message

For what we preach is not ourselves, but Jesus Christ as Lord, and ourselves as your servants for Jesus' sake. For God, who said, "Let light shine out of darkness," made his light shine in our hearts to give us the light of the knowledge of God's glory displayed in the face of Christ.

But we have this treasure in jars of clay to show that this all-surpassing power is from God and not from us.

—2 Corinthians 4:5–7

Open Your Mind
to understand God's message then and now

This passage gives us two strong images that don't seem to go together: dazzling light and ordinary clay pots. Talking about light, Paul went back to creation, back to God's command to "Let there be light" (Genesis 1:3). The light of God now blazes in our hearts.

But we carry the "treasure" of this light in "jars of clay." These are cheap vessels, dirty, easily breakable—and so are we. It's likely that the apostle was thinking back to creation again when God "formed a man from the dust of the ground" (Genesis 2:7). We humans are made from humus, soil, earth. We are, in a quite literal way, clay vessels.

So what's the point? Don't think too highly of yourself. It's not about you. Plant a flower in an earthen pot and no one looks at the pot. But despite our ordinary nature, we have an amazingly important job to do. We are breakable humans bearing the light of God! As we attempt to be the message, it makes no sense to emphasize our skill at message-being. We preach Christ, not ourselves.

Open Your Heart
to the divine whisper

Spend some time in silence considering God's glory and His amazing decision to share it with us. Let gratitude fill your heart. What do you hear Him telling you?

_____

_____

_____

_____

_____

Open Your Life
to God's transforming power

Light and clay come together in one Old Testament story. When Gideon led a small band of three hundred soldiers in a sneak attack on a vast army, he had them bring trumpets, torches, and clay jars. Surrounding the enemy camp at night, they kept the blazing torches inside the jars until Gideon gave the signal. Then they smashed the jars, shouted, and blew the trumpets. Can you imagine the light and sound that suddenly filled that camp? It had the desired effect, sending the enemy army into a panic.

The light appeared only when the clay jars were broken.

Imagine the one soldier who says, "My jar was so beautiful I just couldn't bear to smash it." He's missing the point. And so are we when we take pride in the power of our own testimony. If people are dazzled by the beauty of our gospel presentation, there's something wrong. We are just containers for this treasure of God's light. That's what people need to see, not us. We are made to be broken.

In the verses following today's passage, Paul speaks of his own difficulties in sharing the gospel. He's been "hard pressed . . . persecuted . . . struck down" (verses 8–9). If you face opposition in your efforts to be the message, it doesn't mean you're doing it wrong. On the contrary. That's what lets the light shine through.

What breaking have you experienced in your efforts to shine God's light?

_____

_____

_____

_____

_____

_____

Open Your Arms
to a world that needs to receive God's incarnate message through you

Look for other "jars of clay," like yourself, who might need support or counsel.

If someone is at a breaking point—facing difficulty for serving the Lord—provide loving reassurance. But perhaps others are promoting themselves more than Christ. Is there a way you could lovingly communicate the theme of today's passage from one clay jar to another?

_____

_____

_____

_____

_____

_____

Open Yourself
to a dynamic encounter with God

As you prepare yourself for this time with God, be ready for His surprises.

Open God's Word
to hear God's message

A man was going down from Jerusalem to Jericho, when he was attacked by robbers. They stripped him of his clothes, beat him and went away, leaving him half dead. A priest happened to be going down the same road, and when he saw the man, he passed by on the other side. So too, a Levite, when he came to the place and saw him, passed by on the other side. But a Samaritan, as he traveled, came where the man was; and when he saw him, he took pity on him. He went to him and bandaged his wounds, pouring on oil and wine. Then he put the man on his own donkey, brought him to an inn and took care of him. The next day he took out two denarii and gave them to the innkeeper. "Look after him," he said, "and when I return, I will reimburse you for any extra expense you may have."

—LUKE 10:30–35

Open Your Mind
to understand God's message then and now

It's hard for us to imagine how shocking the story of the Good Samaritan was to Jesus's audience.

A lawyer had a question about the biblical command to "love your neighbor as yourself" (verse 27). Perhaps looking for a loophole, he asked Jesus to define *neighbor*. In response Jesus told the now-familiar parable.

Surprisingly, the "good guys"—the priest and the Levite—leave the needy man by the side of the road. The person who shows love is one of the Samaritans, a group generally despised and distrusted by the Jews of that day.

We might expect a story in which the Samaritan is the needy one. The question would be, which of the passersby would overlook the cultural boundaries and help him out? But Jesus turned things around. It was the Samaritan who crossed the ethnic divide and treated the needy Jew as his neighbor, *not* the two Jews who shared a bloodline with the man.

Scripture does not allow us to pick and choose which neighbors to love. Anyone we walk past is a neighbor, whether or not the person shares our race, religion, or anything else, and we should be neighborly.

Open Your Heart
to the divine whisper

Lord, break through my assumptions. Teach me a new way of thinking, a new way of seeing. Show me new ways to honor you.

_____

_____

_____

_____

Open Your Life
to God's transforming power

There's no doubt about it: love is job number one for Christians. Loving God and loving others—that's what God's law boils down to. Even in a scrimmage with faith and hope, the greatest is love.

So as Christians, we devote ourselves to love, but too often we set limits on it. We agree to love others as long as it doesn't cost too much. As long as it won't be a longstanding commitment. As long as it doesn't put us at risk. As long as we can stay within our own group. Love is a great idea, but let's not get crazy about it.

That was pretty much the attitude of the priest and the Levite. They were probably big fans of love as an idea, but they set very narrow limits on its practice. The Samaritan, on the other hand, went over and above any reasonable limits. His love cost him money, time, and effort.

Crazy, yes, but that's love.

What kinds of limits have you placed on loving others? How would God like you to revise those limitations?

_____

_____

_____

_____

_____

Open Your Arms
to a world that needs to receive God's incarnate message through you

We're especially impressed with the *time* this Samaritan took to meet this need. In our busy lives time might be a more valuable commodity than money. We hurry from activity to activity without seeing the needs around us. Even if we do, there's no time to stop and get involved.

Here's a thought: budget some time in your schedule for the specific purpose of helping others. An hour or two a week. One night every month. A Saturday per quarter. You can figure out the details, but try to block it out as firmly as if it were an important meeting at work.

Then be alert to the needs around you. If you don't find enough needs to fill that time, then use it to pray and listen for God's whisper. You're being proactive about being the message. You're carving out a time devoted to loving your neighbors.

How would this work in your life?

_____

_____

_____

_____

Open Yourself
to a dynamic encounter with God

> For you are great and do marvelous deeds;
>> you alone are God.
> Teach me your way, LORD,
>> that I may rely on your faithfulness.
>> —Psalm 86:10–11

Open God's Word
to hear God's message

"If we are thrown into the blazing furnace, the God we serve is able to deliver us from it, and he will deliver us from Your Majesty's hand. But even if he does not, we want you to know, Your Majesty, that we will not serve your gods or worship the image of gold you have set up." . . .

Then King Nebuchadnezzar leaped to his feet in amazement and asked his advisers, "Weren't there three men that we tied up and threw into the fire?"

They replied, "Certainly, Your Majesty."

He said, "Look! I see four men walking around in the fire, un-bound and unharmed, and the fourth looks like a son of the gods."

—DANIEL 3:17–18, 24–25

Open Your Mind
to understand God's message then and now

The Babylonian conquest of Judah occurred in three waves. In the first, around 605 BC, the most promising young men were carted off to Babylon to be groomed as leaders, including Daniel and his three friends. Why enslave such talent when you can co-opt it?

The early chapters of the book of Daniel show us how these four Jews fared in this foreign court. They caused a stir by rejecting the rich food offered to them, but they earned high marks in health, learning, and the interpretation of dreams. Daniel attained a high position in the government of King Nebuchadnezzar, and administrative posts were given to Shadrach, Meshach, and Abednego.

But then the king conducted a test of loyalty. He set up a huge statue of himself and required everyone to bow before it. Apparently Daniel was elsewhere at the time, but his three friends refused to bow. As punishment, they were thrown into a blazing furnace.

They survived without a singe, and in one of the Old Testament's great Christ-sightings, the king declared that he saw a fourth figure— "like a son of the gods"—in the furnace. As Christians, we have little doubt that it was in fact the Son of God who stood with those faithful youths in their fiery ordeal.

In response to the event, the king himself said, "Praise be to the God of Shadrach, Meshach and Abednego" (verse 28).

Open Your Heart
to the divine whisper

Think about the times the Lord has delivered you from danger. What courage will He require of you in the future? Listen for His challenge.

_____

_____

_____

_____

_____

_____

Open Your Life
to God's transforming power

The Babylonians tried to assimilate Daniel and his friends by wooing them into the new kingdom, bribing them with tasty food, and making them want to fit in. Yet from the start the Hebrew youths resisted the wooing and maintained their identity. When it came time to bow to a statue, they had the strength to say no and the courage to face the consequences.

If someone put an idol in front of you and said, "Worship it," you'd find it easy to say no. But modern idols are usually less obvious. Without knowing it, we slide into the worship of money, beauty, or celebrity. The world assimilates us, bribing us with various pleasures and making us want to fit in. It's hard to know where the idolatry starts, but at some point we can forget who we really are.

Ironically, Nebuchadnezzar's loyalty test turned out to be a test of the Hebrews' loyalty to God, which they passed with flaming colors. Maybe we ought to test our own loyalty at times. Who or what are we really serving?

How can you stop the slide into idolatry and show your full devotion to God?

_____

_____

_____

_____

_____

Open Your Arms
to a world that needs to receive God's incarnate message through you

Did Abednego have second thoughts? Did Shadrach have to encourage him? We don't know the inner workings of that trio, only that they acted together. We assume there must have been mutual support.

There are people around you who need support like that. Perhaps they are sliding into idolatry of one sort or another. Perhaps you can remind them that there's one true God worth worshiping.

This is not a matter of snooping and judging. You don't want to be looking over other people's shoulders and critiquing their spiritual lives. *You're getting a bit too worshipful about that football team, aren't you?* No. But God will bring to your mind certain friends who need support. You can share with them your own struggle to stay true to the Lord in a world of idols. What friends is God bringing to mind?

_____

_____

_____

_____

_____

Open Yourself
to a dynamic encounter with God

Close your eyes and focus your attention on the invisible God. Are you ready for Him to teach you a new way of seeing?

Open God's Word
to hear God's message

"For I was hungry and you gave me something to eat, I was thirsty and you gave me something to drink, I was a stranger and you invited me in, I needed clothes and you clothed me, I was sick and you looked after me, I was in prison and you came to visit me."

Then the righteous will answer him, "Lord, when did we see you hungry and feed you, or thirsty and give you something to drink? When did we see you a stranger and invite you in, or needing clothes and clothe you? When did we see you sick or in prison and go to visit you?"

The King will reply, "Truly I tell you, whatever you did for one of the least of these brothers and sisters of mine, you did for me."

—MATTHEW 25:35–40

Open Your Mind
to understand God's message then and now

It's a strange story with a life-changing punch line. One of Jesus's more elaborate parables and one that raises more questions than it answers, yet it engraves an image deep in our hearts.

The central figure is called the Son of Man, a title Jesus often used for Himself. He's also called "the King," and He acts like a shepherd dividing sheep from goats. That sounds confusing, but it's all the same person. Son of Man = King = Shepherd = Jesus.

He rewards some for meeting His needs and judges others harshly because they ignored Him. Both sides are confused. When did they ever see Him in need? And then Jesus delivered the life-changing answer: *Whatever they did for the lowest members of society, they did for the Son of Man.*

So in a very real way, Jesus is the beggar on the street. He is not only the Son of Man and the King, but He is also the needy person we choose to help—or not.

Open Your Heart
to the divine whisper

In the silence let the Lord bring before you images of "the least of these brothers and sisters" of His who are in need. How does He want you to respond?

_____

_____

_____

_____

_____

_____

_____

_____

Open Your Life
to God's transforming power

Through the ages various storytellers have used this device: the king dresses as a beggar and roams through the kingdom to see how things really are. Everybody will treat a king with respect, of course, but how are beggars treated? In Jesus's story the sheep reveal their true hearts by caring for the poor with no expectation of reward. They are surprised and delighted when the Son of Man rewards them.

We often think of charity as a matter of digging into our excess resources to help the unfortunate have-nots, something that moral people do. It feels good.

But Jesus turns the whole transaction on its head by identifying with the needy. In a way the beggar is doing us a favor by allowing us to show love to Christ. Helping the needy is not a duty but a privilege. And if the poor are, in Mother Teresa's words, "Jesus in disguise," then charity becomes a sacred relationship, an act of worship, a transaction of love.

The New Testament makes it clear that you simply cannot love the Lord without loving others (see 1 John 4:19–21). This parable teaches us that we show love to the Lord *by* loving others.

Does this challenge or change your idea of charity? If so, how?

_____

_____

_____

_____

_____

Open Your Arms
to a world that needs to receive God's incarnate message through you

Give more.

That's the challenge you expect here, isn't it? We all can dig deeper to help the needy, but there's more to this parable.

See more.

Jesus calls the needy His "brothers and sisters." We help Him by helping them. Can you see Jesus in the homeless vet, the terminal patient, the strung-out addict? Our giving has to start with seeing.

Give more of yourself.

Charity has to be more than a line in a checkbook. It will cost us more to get involved, but that's what is required. Work in a downtown soup kitchen, and get to know the people who come through. Tutor poor kids. Join a prison outreach. There are many good ministries involved in helping the needy. Most are crying out for volunteers.

If these needy souls are Jesus in disguise, we need to love them, not just fund them.

How can you get involved? What ministries is God bringing to your heart? Can you call someone tomorrow to start the process?

_____

_____

_____

_____

_____

Open Yourself
to a dynamic encounter with God

In the stillness prepare yourself for action. Attend to the Lord fully and carefully, and then get ready to follow His lead.

Open God's Word
to hear God's message

"Let's go across to the outpost of those pagans," Jonathan said to his armor bearer. "Perhaps the LORD will help us, for nothing can hinder the LORD. He can win a battle whether he has many warriors or only a few!"

"Do what you think is best," the armor bearer replied. "I'm with you completely, whatever you decide." . . .

"Come on, climb right behind me," Jonathan said to his armor bearer, "for the LORD will help us defeat them!"

So they climbed up using both hands and feet, and the Philistines fell before Jonathan, and his armor bearer killed those who came behind them.

—1 SAMUEL 14:6–7, 12–13, NLT

Open Your Mind
to understand God's message then and now

The Israelites and the Philistines carried on an extensive conflict in the period of the judges and the early monarchy, which was roughly

1100–1000 BC. Based by the sea, the Philistines had better access to the latest technology, like iron weapons, but the Israelites were scrappy, and they defended their hill country well.

In this passage Saul is king. His son Jonathan is a military commander. The Philistines are winning the war, sending raiding parties throughout Israelite territory. Oddly, King Saul is doing nothing.

Suddenly Jonathan has a crazy secret plan: a daring attack on an enemy outpost. The plan is so secret he doesn't even tell his father. The plan is so crazy it involves only him and his armor bearer—two of them engaging an army. "Perhaps the LORD will help us," says Jonathan. *There's* a pep talk for you. Kudos to the armor bearer for going along with it.

The two men climb up a cliff to confront the Philistine guards, who clearly see them coming. There's not even an element of surprise! But Jonathan and his unnamed assistant fight valiantly and win. This demoralizes the rest of the Philistine army. Oh, yes, and there's an earthquake that terrifies them even more. The enemy retreats. Israel wins the day, thanks to a prince's bravado, a servant's unquestioning loyalty, and a well-timed earthquake.

Open Your Heart
to the divine whisper

Be honest about your hesitations and concerns, but keep listening to His urging. How is this conversation going?

_____

_____

_____

_____

_____

_____

Open Your Life
to God's transforming power

Jonathan seems to be operating out of what we call a "holy disturbance." He's unhappy with the fact that the Philistines are sweeping
through the land. It's just *wrong* to see God's country defiled like that.
He needs to do something and soon.

Jesus told a story about three servants entrusted with their master's money. Two invested it and reaped the benefits. But a third servant was afraid of losing it, so he buried it in the ground. Sometimes
we're like that third servant, afraid of doing something wrong, so we
don't do anything.

Jonathan acts. He believes that God gave him the holy disturbance to begin with, and he trusts God to help him.

Is God encouraging you to take action in some matter? Is He
giving you a holy disturbance? Is there some "crazy" plan He keeps
bringing to your thoughts? What is He telling you now about that?

_____

_____

_____

_____

_____

_____

Open Your Arms
to a world that needs to receive God's incarnate message through you

What's your holy disturbance? Is there something you see that needs to change? Some need that keeps crying out to you? Make sure this is a *holy* disturbance and not just your own pet peeve. Beware of pride and judgment. This is not an excuse to tear down other people.

If your prompting is genuinely coming from the Lord, then *discuss with Him what you can do about it.* This is the time for "crazy" ideas. Can you start a new ministry? Can you quit your job and work for a charity? Can you go on a mission trip? Can you launch a website, make a video, circulate a petition, run for office? Brainstorm these things with the Lord. Don't rule anything out just yet. Even in the most far-fetched ideas, "perhaps the LORD will help" you.

Take a first step. Many of our best intentions never become realities because we never act on them. So make a call. Talk to someone. Sign up. Get some info.

Find your armor bearer. There are few lone rangers in effective ministry. We need others to support us, to challenge us, to hone the vision. So talk with people about your holy disturbance and the steps you're taking. Maybe nine of them will say, "That's crazy," but the tenth one might become a valued teammate.

How's your "crazy" idea shaping up?

_____

_____

_____

_____

Open Yourself
to a dynamic encounter with God

As the heavens are higher than the earth,
    so are my ways higher than your ways
    and my thoughts than your thoughts.
—Isaiah 55:9

Open God's Word
to hear God's message

Brothers and sisters, think of what you were when you were called. Not many of you were wise by human standards; not many were influential; not many were of noble birth. But God chose the foolish things of the world to shame the wise; God chose the weak things of the world to shame the strong. God chose the lowly things of this world and the despised things—and the things that are not—to nullify the things that are, so that no one may boast before him. It is because of him that you are in Christ Jesus, who has become for us wisdom from God—that is, our righteousness, holiness and redemption. Therefore, as it is written: "Let the one who boasts boast in the Lord."

—1 Corinthians 1:26–31

Open Your Mind
to understand God's message then and now

In a world that puffs up the importance of social status, the church puts everyone on equal footing. It doesn't matter how rich or well educated we are; we are all sinners saved by grace. It's not what we know or even who we know; it's whether we know Jesus.

The apostle Paul spells it out early in his letter to the contentious Corinthians. That church had people elbowing each other for prominence, the rich looking down on the poor, different leaders fighting for bragging rights, and new preachers coming to town questioning Paul's education. Just when we would expect Paul to assert his authority as the church's founder, he does the opposite. There are no bragging rights. We have nothing to boast about, except the Lord.

We're not wise or influential or noble, he says. This is not a church of movers and shakers; we're just moved and shaken by God, who routinely chooses the lesser over the greater. Young David felled a giant. Gideon's tiny band of trumpeters beat an army. A peasant girl bore the Christ child. The Lord doesn't care about human status. He wants our openness. Will we let Him do His work through us?

Open Your Heart
to the divine whisper

Lord, You know who I am and who I'm not. You know what I can do and what I can't. Truth is, I can do nothing without You. Show me how to serve You.

_____

_____

_____

_____

_____

_____

_____

_____

_____

_____

Open Your Life
to God's transforming power

Perhaps you find yourself saying, "If only I were richer, then I could give to God's work." Or "If I were more of a leader, I could start the ministry I've been thinking about." Or "I'm not very skilled at speaking, so how can I share the gospel with people?" If so, you're making assumptions on the basis of the way the world works, but that's not how God works. If you feel you don't have what it takes to serve Him, well, that's exactly the qualification He's looking for. As the scripture says, God chooses the weak, the lowly, the insignificant people of the world to shine for Him.

As the world of Christian media has grown in recent times, a success culture has grown with it, along with an assortment of unhelpful attitudes. "If only my music could be played in the megachurches." "If only I could get on that TV show." "If only I could write a bestseller." "If only my John 3:16 selfie could go viral." *Then* I could reach the world for God.

What does today's passage from 1 Corinthians say about that?

What sort of "if only" thinking have you been doing? How does God want you to serve Him now, where you are?

_____

_____

_____

_____

_____

Open Your Arms
to a world that needs to receive God's incarnate message through you

Imagine: if you were wiser, more influential, or more talented, how would you use those abilities to serve the Lord? Would you find a new way to meet a need in your community? Would you go overseas to spread the gospel in a region you care about?

Well, what's stopping you? The Lord doesn't need stars. He needs you, serving Him with whatever you bring to the table. Gather some others around you, and let God do His work through you.

Where will you start?

_____

_____

_____

_____

_____

Open Yourself
to a dynamic encounter with God

Rest today in the amazing love of God. "No power in the sky above or in the earth below—indeed, nothing in all creation will ever be able to separate us from the love of God that is revealed in Christ Jesus our Lord" (Romans 8:39, NLT).

Open God's Word
to hear God's message

This is how we know what love is: Jesus Christ laid down his life for us. And we ought to lay down our lives for our brothers and sisters. If anyone has material possessions and sees a brother or sister in need but has no pity on them, how can the love of God be in that person? Dear children, let us not love with words or speech but with actions and in truth.

—1 JOHN 3:16–18

Open Your Mind
to understand God's message then and now

In his first epistle John deals with the big themes of Christianity: life, light, truth, and, most of all, love. He seems especially interested in verification. *How do we know Christianity is true?*

That makes sense. There were false teachers twisting the message of Christ into all sorts of heresies. "Test the spirits," John tells his readers, "to see whether they are from God" (4:1). "This is how you know," he keeps saying. Truth is a precious commodity, and he wants to preserve it.

So under the surface of this "love letter," a battle is going on. John fights for a proper understanding of who Jesus is and how He continues to affect believers' lives. How do we know what love is? Look at Jesus dying for us. Do you want to show love for others? Die for them. Any more questions? John doesn't mince words. Christian love is serious stuff.

What if you see someone in need, and what if you have what he needs? If the love of God is in you, how can you withhold that from him? Love requires sacrifice. It's easy to talk about love, but this is how we actually love.

Open Your Heart
to the divine whisper

Lord, I spend a lot of time trying to close my heart to the needs around me, not because I'm unkind, but just to keep my sanity. There's a lot of need out there. I ask You to pry open my heart. Show me what I need to see. And help me deal with all of it.

_____

_____

_____

_____

_____

Open Your Life
to God's transforming power

It's worth noting that John's instruction has to do with loving other *Christians*. At this point Rome was cracking down on the church, so there was persecution and discrimination. Many Christians were in great need. John reminds his readers that we need to care for our spiritual family.

Years earlier John had heard Jesus say, "By this everyone will know that you are my disciples, if you love one another" (John 13:35). Love shown within the church would be a testimony to the truth of Christ's message. It's not that we turn off the love when dealing with nonbelievers. It's just that there is a special bond with those who share our faith in Christ. And when a high level of need arises within the church, we must put love into action.

What particular needs are you aware of within your local church or among other Christians around the world? What can you do to help?

_____

_____

_____

_____

_____

_____

_____

_____

_____

Open Your Arms
to a world that needs to receive God's incarnate message through you

In many countries of the world, Christians are suffering greatly. Some face persecution; others are in war zones; still others are dealing with crushing poverty or reeling from recent disasters. You personally can't fix all those problems, but you can join with the international community of Christians to ease the burden.

Perhaps your church or denomination is connected to an international organization for persecuted churches or some other relief agency. In some poor areas churches need books and resources, including Bibles. They need funding to educate church leaders. Sometimes people just need economic opportunity. We have been supporting Haitian coffee growers by providing a fair market in America for their product. There are also groups that provide microloans for artisans and small businesses in poor regions. Use the creativity and passion God has given you to meet the needs you become aware of.

Keep in mind that there is already a worldwide network devoted to loving people. We call it the church. Local churches in these regions will probably be valuable teammates as you seek to provide the resources they lack. What particular needs could you help meet?

_____

_____

_____

_____

_____

_____

Open Yourself
to a dynamic encounter with God

Do you enjoy this special time with the Lord? If it has become drudgery, stop and start over. Seriously. Come back at a time when you can relax in the presence of the best Friend you've ever had.

Open God's Word
to hear God's message

Then Peter, filled with the Holy Spirit, said to them: "Rulers and elders of the people! If we are being called to account today for an act of kindness shown to a man who was lame and are being asked how he was healed, then know this, you and all the people of Israel: It is by the name of Jesus Christ of Nazareth, whom you crucified but whom God raised from the dead, that this man stands before you healed." . . .

When they saw the courage of Peter and John and realized that they were unschooled, ordinary men, they were astonished and they took note that these men had been with Jesus. But since they could see the man who had been healed standing there with them, there was nothing they could say.

—Acts 4:8–10, 13–14

Open Your Mind
to understand God's message then and now

Life must have been crazy for those first disciples after the Spirit's Pentecost arrival. Their gathering suddenly grew from 120 to more than 3,000. Small-group meetings were held in homes, classes were conducted in side rooms of the temple complex, and the apostles were out on the street healing people . . . and getting arrested for it.

Peter and John were jailed overnight after healing a lame man in Jesus's name. Standing before the same council that had condemned Jesus about two months earlier, they answered for their "crime" and in the process delivered yet another gospel message.

The authorities didn't like it, but what could they do? The well-known beggar, formerly lame, was standing right there, probably still jumping for joy. Peter and John were reprimanded, released, and ordered not to speak about Jesus anymore.

Yeah, like that was going to happen! In the next chapter we find the apostles back out there, talking with people about Jesus.

It surprised these leaders that Peter and John were so "unschooled" and "ordinary." They were fishermen from Galilee, not the upper crust of Jerusalem. How could they be at the helm of this growing movement? Then "they took note that these men had been with Jesus."

That's our story too, isn't it? We may all lack the skills necessary to change the world. We may be quite ordinary ourselves. But that doesn't matter. The important thing is that we have been with Jesus. Whatever we are, whatever we do, it's because of Him. Let's see what miracles can happen.

Open Your Heart
to the divine whisper

As the Spirit wafts through our lives, we can pray in the words of the old hymn: "Melt me, mold me, fill me, use me." Make that prayer your own.

_____

_____

_____

_____

_____

Open Your Life
to God's transforming power

Being with Jesus. That's what this time is all about, right? You might get educated or inspired, but that's not the purpose here. You are carving this time out of your schedule to *be with Jesus*.

It's a date in a way. Two people spending time together, sharing thoughts, hopes, and dreams. You are getting to know Him better.

Have you ever noticed how couples start acting the same way? They start to share certain mannerisms and phrases, and they have the same timing. It's no surprise that this would happen when they spend so much time together. It's the same thing with you and Jesus. The more time you spend with Him, the more you pick up His instincts. A situation occurs and you react the way He would. You make a helpful comment to a friend and realize it's exactly what He would have said. You start to go through life seeing people with His eyes.

Okay, sometimes you have to make a conscious effort to act in a Christlike way, but after spending so much time with Him, you will find yourself doing this naturally. You know His voice. You're used to taking His advice.

Like Peter and John, you could be "unschooled, ordinary," but when you have "been with Jesus," that changes everything.

How has Jesus been changing you in your time together?

_____

_____

_____

_____

_____

_____

Open Your Arms
to a world that needs to receive God's incarnate message through you

Consider telling someone else about the blessings of your time with Jesus. Be careful that it doesn't sound like bragging about your own spiritual discipline. But see if you can encourage this friend to meet with the Lord in a similar way.

Who might this person be? What would you tell him about?

_____

_____

_____

_____

_____

_____

Open Yourself
to a dynamic encounter with God

Perhaps you have some device in your car or phone that tells you where you are, where you're headed, and where to turn in order to get where you're going. That's sort of what this time with the Lord is. Thank Him for His guidance.

Open God's Word
to hear God's message

> Let love and faithfulness never leave you;
>> bind them around your neck,
>> write them on the tablet of your heart. . . .
> Trust in the LORD with all your heart
>> and lean not on your own understanding;
> in all your ways submit to him,
>> and he will make your paths straight.
>> —Proverbs 3:3, 5–6

Open Your Mind
to understand God's message then and now

Proverbs was written as spiritual training for young men. That's why there's so much emphasis on heeding parents' instruction. That's also why there are warnings about loose women. Fortunately, there is enough practical wisdom in this book to instruct older readers too, male and female alike.

The fear of the Lord is a common theme. Proverbs calls it "the beginning of knowledge" (1:7). It seems appropriate in a handbook for youth to begin at the beginning. And if you've ever dealt with misbehaving kids, you know that fear is a good place to start. But surely we don't need to end there.

In the New Testament, John states that "perfect love drives out fear" (1 John 4:18). "Perfect" has the sense of being fully developed, mature. This helps us put things in place. The journey of faith indeed begins with the fear of the Lord. He is God and we're not. If we don't live His way, things will go badly, so we want to stay on His good side.

But as our journey continues, that high regard for God turns into love. We are awestruck by His amazing love for us, and we love Him in return. We are motivated by our love for Him rather than the fear of Him.

And love is the incubator for *trust*. We trust in His power (He can fulfill His promises), in His wisdom (He knows what is best for us—better than we do), and also in His love (He *wants* what is best for us). That puts us on a straight path to maturity.

Open Your Heart
to the divine whisper

I am in awe of You, Lord. Your power is awesome. But I am also melted by Your love. I trust that You want what's best for me. How can I act on that trust?

_____

_____

_____

_____

_____

Open Your Life
to God's transforming power

The fear of the Lord is a good thing. It makes sense to realize how powerful He is, how much He cares about His creation, and what He requires of us. He is an awesome God.

Some people get stuck in the fear, however. They're careful to do everything right, to perform all their religious duties properly so the Lord won't be upset with them. They never really grow into a loving relationship with God. Their faith is a matter of obligation more than adoration.

The book of Proverbs starts us out nicely with the fear of God, but the New Testament writers (and a number of the prophets) appeal to our hearts too. He is indeed awesome, but He's also, well, *awesome* in the modern sense of that word. He amazes us, surprises us, delights us, and loves us. In response, we love Him back. We don't cower in fear of doing something amiss. We open our hearts to Him, giving all we have just to please Him, not because we're afraid He'll strike us down, but because we long to make Him happy. And we trust that He will lead us in the best possible direction.

How would you characterize your relationship with God? Is it more fear than love, more love than fear, or a balance of the two? How does that play out?

_____

_____

_____

_____

Open Your Arms
to a world that needs to receive God's incarnate message through you

In the quietness of this time with God, tell Him how much you love Him. Hear His assurances of His love for you.

Think about a few of your closest relationships: family, dearest friends. Tell God about your love for these people. Hear Him saying how much He loves them too.

Now, in your own way, *entrust* these relationships to Him. Give them over. Stop leaning on your own understanding. Let God lead you as you navigate the challenges.

Our closest relationships are rich, rewarding, and sometimes hard. But if you trust the Lord with each of those connections, He will embrace you both.

What relationships are you offering to Him?

_____

_____

_____

About the Authors

KERRY and CHRIS SHOOK founded Woodlands Church in 1993, and since then it has become a multisite church with more than eighteen thousand in average attendance every weekend.

Kerry and Chris have a worldwide television ministry that broadcasts to a local, national, and international audience. They can be seen by millions in fifty states and more than two hundred countries worldwide.

They have touched thousands of under-resourced people locally and in countries around the world through the missions and ministries of Woodlands Church.

Kerry and Chris have been married for more than thirty years and have four grown children.

Your Life Is the Message

Living out the gospel in the world today is both simple and costly. Kerry and Chris Shook explore that paradox through biblical stories and their own experience of making a decision to live out the gospel in practical ways. Choosing to be the gospel changed their family, church, and personal relationship with God. How might it transform you?

**Read an excerpt from this book
and more at WaterBrookMultnomah.com**